AN EXCERPT FROM

LUKE

VOLUME 4
(CHAPTERS 22:39–24:53)

THE PREACHER'S OUTLINE & SERMON BIBLE®

NEW TESTAMENT

NEW INTERNATIONAL VERSION

25
LMW

Leadership Ministries Worldwide
Chattanooga, TN

DEDICATED

To all the men and women of the world who
preach and teach the Gospel of
our Lord Jesus Christ and
to the Mercy and Grace of God

&

- Demonstrated to us in Christ Jesus our Lord.

  In him we have redemption through his blood, the forgiveness of sins, in accordance with the riches of God's grace." (Ep.1:7)

- Out of the mercy and grace of God, His Word has flowed. Let every person know that God will have mercy upon him, forgiving and using him to fulfill His glorious plan of salvation.

  "For God so loved the world that he gave his one and only Son, that whoever believes in him shall not perish but have eternal life. For God did not send his Son into the world to condemn the world, but to save the world through him" (Jn.3:16-17)

  "This is good, and pleases God our Savior, who wants all men to be saved and to come to a knowledge of the truth." (1 Ti.2:3-4)

7/03

The Preacher's Outline & Sermon Bible®

is written for God's servants to use in their study, teaching, and preaching of God's Holy Word…

- to share the Word of God with the world.
- to help the believer, both minister and layman alike, in his understanding, preaching, and teaching of God's Word.
- to do everything we possibly can to lead men, women, boys and girls to give their hearts and lives to Jesus Christ and to secure the eternal life which He offers.
- to do all we can to minister to the needy of the world.
- to give Jesus Christ His proper place, the place the Word gives Him. Therefore, no work of Leadership Ministries Worldwide will ever be personalized.

ACKNOWLEDGMENTS AND BIBLIOGRAPHY

Every child of God is precious to the Lord and deeply loved. And every child as a servant of the Lord touches the lives of those who come in contact with him or his ministry. The writing ministries of the following servants have touched this work, and we are grateful that God brought their writings our way. We hereby acknowledge their ministry to us, being fully aware that there are many others down through the years whose writings have touched our lives and who deserve mention, but whose names have faded from our memory. May our wonderful Lord continue to bless the ministries of these dear servants—and the ministries of us all—as we diligently labor to reach the world for Christ and to meet the desperate needs of those who suffer so much.

THE GREEK SOURCES

Expositor's Greek Testament, Edited by W. Robertson Nicoll. Grand Rapids, MI: Eerdmans Publishing Co., 1970.

Robertson, A.T. *Word Pictures in the New Testament*. Nashville, TN: Broadman Press, 1930.

Thayer, Joseph Henry. *Greek-English Lexicon of the New Testament*. New York: American Book Co., n.d.

Vincent, Marvin R. *Word Studies in the New Testament*. Grand Rapids, MI: Eerdmans Publishing Co., 1969.

Vine, W.E. *Expository Dictionary of New Testament Words*. Old Tappan, NJ: Fleming H. Revell Co., n.d.

Wuest, Kenneth S. *Word Studies in the Greek New Testament*. Grand Rapids, MI: Eerdmans Publishing Co., 1966.

THE REFERENCE WORKS

Cruden's Complete Concordance of the Old & New Testament. Philadelphia, PA: The John C. Winston Co., 1930.

Josephus, Flavius. *Complete Works*. Grand Rapids, MI: Kregel Publications, 1981.

Lockyer, Herbert. *All the Books and Chapters of the Bible*. Grand Rapids, MI: Zondervan Publishing House, 1966.

_____. *All the Kings and Queens of the Bible*. Grand Rapids, MI: Zondervan Publishing House, 1961.

_____. *All the Men of the Bible*. Grand Rapids, MI: Zondervan Publishing House, 1958.

_____. *All the Miracles of the Bible*. Grand Rapids, MI: Zondervan Publishing House, 1961.

_____. *All the Parables of the Bible*. Grand Rapids, MI: Zondervan Publishing House, 1963.

_____. *The Women of the Bible*. Grand Rapids, MI: Zondervan Publishing House, 1967.

Nave, Orville J. *Nave's Topical Bible*. Nashville, TN: The Southwestern Company. Copyright © by J.B. Henderson, 1921.

The Amplified Bible. Scripture taken from *THE AMPLIFIED BIBLE*, Old Testament copyright © 1965, 1987 by the Zondervan Publishing House. *The Amplified New Testament* copyright © 1958, 1987 by The Lockman Foundation. Used by permission.

The Four Translation New Testament (Including King James, New American Standard, Williams - New Testament in the Language of the People, Beck - New Testament in the Language of Today.) Minneapolis, MN: World Wide Publications.

The New Compact Bible Dictionary, Edited by T. Alton Bryant. Grand Rapids, MI: Zondervan Publishing House, 1967.

The New Thompson Chain Reference Bible. Indianapolis, IN: B.B. Kirkbride Bible Co., Inc., 1964.

THE COMMENTARIES

Barclay, William. *Daily Study Bible Series*. Philadelphia, PA: Westminster Press, Began in 1953.

Bruce, F.F. *The Epistle to the Ephesians*. Westwood, NJ: Fleming H. Revell Co., 1968.

_____. *Epistle to the Hebrews*. Grand Rapids, MI: Eerdmans Publishing Co., 1964.

_____. *The Epistles of John*. Old Tappan, NJ: Fleming H. Revell Co., 1970.

Criswell, W.A. *Expository Sermons on Revelation*. Grand Rapids, MI: Zondervan Publishing House, 1962-66.

Greene, Oliver. *The Epistles of John*. Greenville, SC: The Gospel Hour, Inc., 1966.

_____. *The Epistles of Paul the Apostle to the Hebrews*. Greenville, SC: The Gospel Hour, Inc., 1965.

_____. *The Epistles of Paul the Apostle to Timothy & Titus*. Greenville, SC: The Gospel Hour, Inc., 1964.

_____. *The Revelation Verse by Verse Study*. Greenville, SC: The Gospel Hour, Inc., 1963.

Henry, Matthew. *Commentary on the Whole Bible*. Old Tappan, NJ: Fleming H. Revell Co.

Hodge, Charles. *Exposition on Romans & on Corinthians*. Grand Rapids, MI: Eerdmans Publishing Co., 1972-1973.

Ladd, George Eldon. *A Commentary On the Revelation of John*. Grand Rapids, MI: Eerdmans Publishing Co., 1972-1973.

Leupold, H.C. *Exposition of Daniel*. Grand Rapids, MI: Baker Book House, 1969.

Morris, Leon. *The Gospel According to John*. Grand Rapids, MI: Eerdmans Publishing Co., 1971.

Newell, William R. *Hebrews, Verse by Verse*. Chicago, IL: Moody Press, 1947.

Strauss, Lehman. *Devotional Studies in Galatians & Ephesians*. Neptune, NJ: Loizeaux Brothers, 1957.

_____. *Devotional Studies in Philippians*. Neptune, NJ: Loizeaux Brothers, 1959.

_____. *James, Your Brother*. Neptune, NJ: Loizeaux Brothers, 1956.

_____. *The Book of the Revelation*. Neptune, NJ: Loizeaux Brothers, 1964.

The New Testament & Wycliffe Bible Commentary, Edited by Charles F. Pfeiffer & Everett F. Harrison. New York: The Iverson Associates, 1971. Produced for Moody Monthly. Chicago Moody Press, 1962.

The Pulpit Commentary, Edited by H.D.M. Spence & Joseph S. Exell. Grand Rapids, MI: Eerdmans Publishing Co., 1950.

Thomas, W.H. Griffith. *Hebrews, A Devotional Commentary*. Grand Rapids, MI: Eerdmans Publishing Co., 1970.

_____. *Outline Studies in the Acts of the Apostles*. Grand Rapids, MI: Eerdmans Publishing Co., 1956.

_____. *St. Paul's Epistle to the Romans*. Grand Rapids, MI: Eerdmans Publishing Co., 1946.

_____. *Studies in Colossians & Philemon*. Grand Rapids, MI: Baker Book House, 1973.

Tyndale New Testament Commentaries. Grand Rapids, MI: Eerdmans Publishing Co., Began in 1958.

Walker, Thomas. *Acts of the Apostles*. Chicago, IL: Moody Press, 1965.

Walvoord, John. *The Thessalonian Epistles*. Grand Rapids, MI: Zondervan Publishing House, 1973.

"Woe is unto me, if I preach not the gospel"

(1 Co.9:16)

Dear Friend,

Whether you are teaching or preaching, there are two things you as a communicator must remember:

- **You must have something to say!**
  Preachers and teachers of the Word of God have the most important message in the universe: the Gospel of Jesus Christ. Paul referred to it as "the message of reconciliation." Mankind can have a relationship with God Himself. As you study God's Word using *The Preacher's Outline & Sermon Bible*, you will find a wealth of information. You *will* have something to say!

- **You must communicate your message in a way that people can understand!**
  Can you imagine having God's Word outlined subject by subject and verse by verse? What a wonderful tool! Using *The Preacher's Outline & Sermon Bible*, you will be able to prepare in-depth lessons and messages that can be clearly understood and comprehended. People will leave having the major points of God's Holy Word placed right in front of them.

You now have the opportunity to preach and teach straight from Luke's Gospel, ***The Passion of Jesus***. Begin by telling of "Jesus' Great Agony." Preach through His sufferings, trials, and crucifixion. End your series by proclaiming "The Son of Man's Glory: His Resurrection, and Ascension." It will thrill the hearts of all who hear. They will remember God's Word because you gave them the hook on which to hang their thoughts: the outline points of God's Holy Word. Preach and teach *The Passion of Jesus* in His power!

Your fellow servants at. . .
LEADERSHIP MINISTRIES WORLDWIDE

OUTLINE OF LUKE

Chapters 22:39–24:53

THE PREACHER'S OUTLINE & SERMON BIBLE is *unique*. It differs from all other Study Bibles & Sermon Resource Materials in that every Passage and Subject is outlined right beside the Scripture. When you choose any *Subject* below and turn to the reference, you have not only the Scripture, but you discover the Scripture and Subject *already outlined for you—verse by verse.*

	XI. THE SON OF MAN'S SUFFERINGS: HIS AGONY, TRIALS, AND CRUCIFIXION, 22:39–23:56	41 He withdrew about a stone's throw beyond them, knelt down and prayed, 42 "Father, if you are willing, take this cup from me; yet not my will, but yours be done."	3. The painful weight of Jesus' sufferings, the cup to be drunk[DS2]
	A. Jesus' Great Agony: Bearing Unbelievable Weight, 22:39-46 (Mt.26:36-46; Mk.14:32-42; Jn.18:1; see Heb.5:7-8; 12:3-4)	43 An angel from heaven appeared to him and strengthened him. 44 And being in anguish, he prayed more earnestly, and his sweat was like drops of blood falling to the ground.	4. The awful weight of Jesus' intense agony[DS3] a. Seen in the angel's visit b. Seen in His intense praying c. Seen in His sweat
1. The setting: Mount of Olives[DS1] a. Jesus' custom to withdraw there for prayer b. Jesus' disciples followed	39 Jesus went out as usual to the Mount of Olives, and his disciples followed him.	45 When he rose from prayer and went back to the disciples, he found them asleep, exhausted from sorrow.	
2. The heavy weight of the trial about to be faced by the disciples	40 On reaching the place, he said to them, "Pray that you will not fall into temptation."	46 "Why are you sleeping?" he asked them. "Get up and pray so that you will not fall into temptation."	5. The tragic weight of the disciples' continued weakness

DIVISION XI

THE SON OF MAN'S SUFFERINGS: HIS AGONY, TRIALS, AND CRUCIFIXION, 22:39–23:56

A. Jesus' Great Agony: Bearing Unbelievable Weight, 22:39-46

(22:39-46) **Introduction**: this passage shows the great weight of suffering Jesus underwent in facing the cross.
1. The setting: Jesus on the Mount of Olives (v.39).
2. The heavy weight of the trial about to be faced by the disciples (v.40).
3. The painful weight of Jesus' sufferings, the cup to be drunk (vv.41-42).
4. The awful weight of Jesus' intense agony (vv.43-44).
5. The tragic weight of the disciples' continued weakness (vv.45-46).

1 (22:39) **Prayer—Jesus Christ, Prayer Life of**: Jesus entered the Mount of Olives. His disciples were with Him. The significant thing to note is this: it was His custom to seek time alone with God on the mount when in Jerusalem. During the last week of His life, He was spending every night in prayer (see note 2).

DEEPER STUDY # 1

(21:37) **Mount of Olives or Olivet**: the mountain range was a little more than one-half mile from the city limits of Jerusalem. The range of mountains lie on the east of Jerusalem and stretch only about one or two miles across. The mountain range was loved by Jesus. It was...
• where Jesus often resorted (Lk.22:39).
• where Jesus often spent the night when in Jerusalem (Jn.7:53-8:1).
• where Jesus spent the nights of His last week on earth—praying and seeking God (Lk.29:37).
• where Jesus first went when He approached Jerusalem to face His last week on earth (Mt.21:1f; Mk.11:1f).
• where the great sermon on the end time was preached (Mt.24:3f; Mk.13:3f).
• where (at the descent) the Triumphal Entry began (Lk.19:37f).
• where Jesus' terrible agony in the Garden of Gethsemane took place. The Garden of Gethsemane was on the side of the mountain (Mt.26:30f; Mk.14:26).
• where the ascension took place (Acts 1:12).

2 (22:40) **Jesus Christ, Sufferings—Discipleship**: Jesus bore the weight of His disciples' great trial. The greatest trial the disciples were ever to know was at hand, and they did not know it. In just a few hours they were going to fall away. They desperately needed to pray that they "will not fall into temptation" (v.40), that they not be so gripped by temptation and sin that they would be too weak to repent when Jesus arose and confronted them. Jesus knew the enormous temptation that was coming upon these men, and He loved and cared for them, so He was bound to feel the pressure of their trial.

For we do not have a high priest who is unable to sympathize with our weaknesses, but we have one who has been tempted in every way, just as we are—yet was without sin. Let us then approach the throne of grace with confidence, so that we may receive mercy and find grace to help us in our time of need. (Heb 4:15-16)

For our struggle is not against flesh and blood, but against the rulers, against the authorities, against the powers of this dark world and against the spiritual forces of evil in the heavenly realms. Therefore put on the full armor of God, so that when the day of evil comes, you may be able to stand your ground, and after you have done everything, to stand. (Eph 6:12-13)

1

Therefore, dear friends, since you already know this, be on your guard so that you may not be carried away by the error of lawless men and fall from your secure position. (2 Pet 3:17)

3 (22:41-42) **Jesus Christ, Sufferings**: Jesus bore the weight of His own cup of suffering. In confronting death Jesus turned to God, crying with *loud cries and tears* (see Heb.5:7). Four things are seen in this verse.

1. Jesus got all alone and prostrated Himself before God. Luke says He withdrew "about a stone's throw" from the three disciples. Note two significant points. (1) He needed to be alone with God—He was desperate. (b) He fell on His face—the pressure and weight were unbearable.

2. Jesus prayed, "Father (pater)." It is the address of a child's love and dependency and trust. The child knows that His father will hear and turn to him when he calls "Father." But note also the word, "Father." Jesus was broken and weighted down; He had fallen prostrate on the ground with His face buried in His hands. In desperation He cried out "Father" (see Mt.26:39). Like a child, He cried out to His Father in brokenness and dependency, knowing that His Father would hear Him and turn to help Him.

3. Jesus asked God to take the cup away from Him. (See DEEPER STUDY # 4, Cup—Mt.26:39. Also see DEEPER STUDY #1—Mt.27:26-44; see Mt.20:19.) The human nature and will of Jesus is clearly seen in this experience. He was as much flesh as any man is; therefore, He begged God to choose another way other than the cup, if possible. The experience of being *separated from God* on the cross was too much to bear.

4. The divine nature and will of Jesus is also clearly seen in this experience. Note the Lord's words: "Take this cup from me: yet not my will...." The first act, the first impulse and struggle of His will, had come from His flesh: to escape the cup of separation from God. But immediately, the second act, the second impulse and struggle of His will, came from His Godly nature: not to do as He willed, but as God willed.

Jesus' surrender to do God's perfect will in the Garden of Gethsemane was critical.

⇒ It was in His surrender that He was made perfect and was able to stand before God as the Ideal, Perfect Man.

⇒ It was in His surrender to be the Ideal, Perfect Man that His righteousness was able to stand for every man.

⇒ It was in His surrender to be the Ideal, Perfect Man that He was able to bear the cup of God's wrath against sin *for every man*.

⇒ It was in His surrender to be the Ideal, Perfect Man that His sacrifice and sufferings were able to stand for every man.

But we see Jesus, who was made a little lower than the angels, now crowned with glory and honor because he suffered death, so that by the grace of God he might taste death for everyone. In bringing many sons to glory, it was fitting that God, for whom and through whom everything exists, should make the author of their salvation perfect through suffering. (Heb 2:9-10)

Although he was a son, he learned obedience from what he suffered and,

once made perfect, he became the source of eternal salvation for all who obey him (Heb 5:8-9)

God made him who had no sin to be sin for us, so that in him we might become the righteousness of God. (2 Cor 5:21)

DEEPER STUDY # 2

(22:42) **Cup**: Jesus Christ was not fearing nor shrinking from death itself. This is clearly seen in Jn.10:17-18. Death for a cause is not such a great price to pay. Many men have died for causes fearlessly and willingly, some perhaps even more cruelly than Jesus Himself. Shrinking from betrayal, beatings, humiliation, and death—increased by foreknowledge—is not what was happening to Jesus. As stated, some men have faced such trials courageously, even inviting martyrdom for a cause. The Lord knew He was to die from the very beginning, and He had been preparing His disciples for His death (see DEEPER STUDY # 1—Lk.9:22). It was not human and physical suffering from which Jesus was shrinking. Such an explanation is totally inadequate in explaining Gethsemane. The great cup or trial Jesus was facing was separation from God (see note, pt.1—Mt.26:37-38). He was to be the sacrificial *Lamb of God* who was to take away the sins of the world (Jn.1:29). He was to bear the judgment of God for the sins of the world (see note—Mt.27:46-49; see Is.53:10). Jesus Himself had already spoken of the "cup" when referring to His sacrificial death (see DEEPER STUDY # 2—Mt.20:22-23; note—Mk.14:41-42; DEEPER STUDY # 2—Jn.18:11).

Scripture speaks of the cup in several ways.

1. The cup is called "the cup of His wrath" (Is.51:17).

2. The cup is associated with suffering and God's wrath (see Ps.11:6; Is.51:17; Lk.22:42).

3. The cup is also associated with salvation. Because Jesus drank the cup of suffering and wrath for us, we can "lift up the cup of salvation and call on the name of the Lord" (Ps.116:13). He bears the judgment of God for the sins of the world (Is.53:10).

---

4 (22:43-44) **Jesus Christ, Suffering**: Jesus bore the awful weight of intense agony. This is seen in three facts.

1. God had to send an angel to strengthen Jesus. What did the angel do? We are not told, but certainly the angel would have shared how...

• Christ's death was an act that glorified and honored God because it was doing exactly what His Father wanted. It was an act of obedience, of love and adoration for God. It was an offering, the perfect offering to God (see note—Eph.5:2).

• Christ's death was to result in His own glory and honor and exaltation (Heb.12:2; Ph.2:6-11).

• Christ's death was the only way man could be saved eternally.

Also, the angel probably did some very practical things. We can imagine the angel embracing his Lord, holding Christ ever so tightly, perhaps infusing strength into His being. The scene of our Lord's being so weak that He had to be embraced and engulfed in the arms of an angel should break the believer's heart. Perhaps the angel wiped the perspiration and blood and tears off His brow. Whatever the scene, we need to see the awful weight and intensity of our Lord's agony.

2. He prayed "more earnestly," more intensely. The reason is seen in the Greek words for "being in anguish"

(genomenos en agonia). The Greek (aorist participle) means Jesus experienced a growing agony. The weight on Him was not only intense, it grew more and more intense. The pressure of suffering became heavier and heavier. The picture is that of His becoming engrossed and embodied in agony. Thus, He prayed more and more earnestly. His prayer grew and increased in intensity even as His agony intensified.

3. He sweat drops like blood. The words "drops of blood" (thromboi) mean thick clots of blood. Apparently Jesus was under so much pressure the capillary veins right under the skin burst and the blood mingled with sweat and poured through the enlarged pores. What Jesus was experiencing can never be known (see DEEPER STUDY # 2, *Jesus Christ, Suffering*—Lk.22:43-44).

DEEPER STUDY # 3

(22:43-44) **Jesus Christ, Suffering**: words could never express what Jesus experienced. Words to describe the suffering of Jesus are totally inadequate. Attempting to describe the agony Jesus felt would be as inadequate as using a syringe to drain an ocean.

1. There was the *mental and emotional agony*: the weight, pressure, anguish, sorrow, and excessive strain such as no man has ever experienced. He was the Son of God, the Maker of heaven and earth; but *now* pressing in ever so heavily upon His mind and spirit were the images, the thoughts of...

- the *hardness and unbelief* of all men everywhere.
- the *rejection* of His own people, the Jews.
- the *malice* of the world's leaders, both Jew and Gentile, religious and civil.
- the *betrayal* of one of His own, Judas.
- the *desertion* of all His disciples.
- the *denial* by the leader of His own men, Peter.
- the *injustice and condemnation* of His trial.
- the *ridicule and pain* of being scourged, spit upon, slugged, cursed, mocked, crowned with thorns, nailed to the cross, and killed.
- the *wrath of God* that was soon to be cast upon Him as the Sin-Bearer of the world, which was by far the heaviest weight of His suffering
- the *departure of God's Spirit* from Him as He bore the sins of the world.

2. There was the *physical experience of death while being the Son of God*. What was it like for the Son of God to die like all men die? If just the physical aspect of Jesus' death is considered, His death was still different from all other men.

a. Jesus as the Son of God possessed the very seed of life within His being (see DEEPER STUDY # 1—Jn.17:2-3).

b. Jesus as the Son of God possessed no seed of death (Jn.14:6; 1 Tim.6:16; 1 Jn.1:1-2. See Jn.1:4.) But man does. Man possesses the seed of corruption and death; man's sinful nature knows nothing and expects nothing but death. However, the sinless nature of Jesus knew nothing of sin and death. Therefore, the agony and pain of death was bound to be as different from man's death as white is different from black.

There is another fact to note as well. Man suffers the depth of humiliation in death. No matter how much man struggles to live, he irrevocably wastes away until he is carried into the grave and dust of the ground. But not Jesus. Again He was sinless, perfect even in His human nature. Imagine the humiliation: the Son of God—Perfect Man,

Perfect God—having to die on this earth! No wonder He "began to be sorrowful and troubled!" (Mt.26:37) No wonder He could say, "My soul is overwhelmed with sorrow, to the point of death" (Mk.14:34). In some mysterious way, God made Jesus to become sin for us (2 Co.5:21).

3. There was *the spiritual experience of death* while being the Son of Man (see note—Mt.5:17-18; DEEPER STUDY # 3—8:20; DEEPER STUDY # 2—Ro.8:3). There is so much in this fact, yet so little ever can be known.

a. First, what is it like to be without sin? Although being fully man, Jesus was sinless. He lived as all men live facing all the trials and temptations that men face, yet He never sinned. He became the Perfect Man, the Ideal Man—all that God wants man to be. Therefore, He became the Pattern for all men.

> **For we do not have a high priest who is unable to sympathize with our weaknesses, but we have one who has been tempted in every way, just as we are—yet was without sin. (Heb 4:15; see 2 Cor.5:21; 1 Pt.2:22; 1 Jn.3:5)**
>
> **Although he was a son, he learned obedience from what he suffered (Heb 5:8)**
>
> **And, once made perfect, he became the source of eternal salvation for all who obey him (Heb 5:9)**

b. Second, what is it like to bear all the sins of the world? What is it like to be perfect and sinless, and then *all of a sudden* to have all the sins of the world laid upon Oneself? In some mysterious way, God took all the sins of the world and laid the whole *body of sin* upon Jesus. God made Jesus to become sin for us (2 Cor.5:21). Jesus, as the Ideal Man, became the Ideal Sin-Bearer. He bore all the sins and all that sin causes, all the...

• darkness	• worry
• pollution	• guilt
• filth	• savagery
• dirt	• conflict
• poison	• consumption
• weight	• strife
• pressure	• warring
• anxiety	• torture
• turmoil	• enmity
• corrosion	• disturbance

> **We all, like sheep, have gone astray, each of us has turned to his own way; and the Lord has laid on him the iniquity of us all. (Isa 53:6)**
>
> **You see, at just the right time, when we were still powerless, Christ died for the ungodly. (Rom 5:6)**
>
> **God made him who had no sin to be sin for us, so that in him we might become the righteousness of God. (2 Cor 5:21)**
>
> **So Christ was sacrificed once to take away the sins of many people; and he will appear a second time, not to bear sin, but to bring salvation to those who are waiting for him. (Heb 9:28)**
>
> **He himself bore our sins in his body on the tree, so that we might die to sins and live for righteousness; by his wounds you have been healed. (1 Pet 2:24)**

3

c. Third, what is it like to bear all the condemnation of sin for all men? What is it like to be judged and condemned for *all the sins ever committed*? Jesus suffered for the sins of *the whole world*, suffered *separation* from God. The terrifying mystery of this hellish experience is seen in His cry on the cross, "My God, My God, why have you forsaken me?" (See notes—Mt.27:26-44; 27:46-49; 1 Pt.2:21-25.)

> But he was pierced for our transgressions, he was crushed for our iniquities; the punishment that brought us peace was upon him, and by his wounds we are healed. (Isa 53:5)
> Christ redeemed us from the curse of the law by becoming a curse for us, for it is written: "Cursed is everyone who is hung on a tree." (Gal 3:13)
> But we see Jesus, who was made a little lower than the angels, now crowned with glory and honor because he suffered death, so that by the grace of God he might taste death for everyone. (Heb 2:9)
> For Christ died for sins once for all, the righteous for the unrighteous, to bring you to God. He was put to death in the body but made alive by the Spirit, (1 Pet 3:18)

5 (22:45-46) **Jesus Christ, Suffering**: Jesus bore the weight of the disciples' continued weakness. The disciples were weak, so weak in fact that they were of no help to Jesus as He faced the most severe crises of His life. Jesus had to face the cross knowing the terrible weakness of His own men. Note what happened.

1. Jesus arose from prayer and went to the three who were supposed to be praying with Him. They were asleep. The companionship and spirit of prayer and comfort He had sought were not there. All were asleep. He had been left alone to wrestle with God by Himself.

2. Jesus warned them of temptation. They had failed to pray for Him, but they must not fail to pray for themselves. Jesus said, "Get up and pray." Both were important. *Watchfulness* sees and *praying* prepares. They must watch in order to see temptation coming, and they must pray in order to be prepared when temptation struck.

3. Jesus warned of the flesh and its weakness. They were sleeping because of the emotional strain and distress of the evening. As Luke says, they slept because of "sorrow," that is, sadness (Lk.22:45). The evening had been shocking and taxing. They were weary, fatigued, and preoccupied. Concentration in prayer was difficult. They probably fought to stay awake and to pray for their Lord, but the importance of prayer and of spiritual dependency upon God in facing trials had not yet been learned. They were making two mistakes common among believers.

a. They were depending upon their own wisdom and strength instead of God's Spirit to fight whatever battles lay ahead.

b. They were taking God's deliverance for granted instead of assuring themselves of His deliverance through the testimony of prayer. They believed Christ to be the Messiah; therefore, they believed that God was going to deliver them from the Romans no matter what. As carnal, fleshy men are apt to do, the disciples no doubt thought prayer mattered little. They were just presuming upon God, taking His deliverance for granted. What Jesus said was, "Watch and pray, for only as you watch and pray can you keep from falling when the trial comes."

A point needs to be noted here: watchfulness and prayer bear *testimony* to God. When men watch and pray, they demonstrate that dependency and trust in God are well founded. When God answers the prayers of men, He demonstrates that He loves and delivers those who truly look up to Him. Without watching and praying, God allows the disciples to fall in order to teach that dependency and trust in Him are absolutely essential.

4. They were failing to stay awake to pray, to watch and be watchful in prayer. Their spirits were not alive and alert enough to overcome the flesh. The drowsiness and slumber of the flesh were stronger than the spirit (see note, pt.2—Mt.26:42-44; see Eph.6:18).

> "Watch and pray so that you will not fall into temptation. The spirit is willing, but the body is weak." (Mat 26:41)
> So, if you think you are standing firm, be careful that you don't fall! (1 Cor 10:12)
> Devote yourselves to prayer, being watchful and thankful. (Col 4:2)
> Be self-controlled and alert. Your enemy the devil prowls around like a roaring lion looking for someone to devour. (1 Pet 5:8)

	B. Jesus' Arrest: Terrible Sins Against Jesus, 22:47-53 (Mt.26:47-56; Mk.14:43-52; Jn.18:3-11)	50 And one of them struck the servant of the high priest, cutting off his right ear.	b. One disciple began fighting
1. Deserting Jesus: The betrayer's sin a. A professing disciple b. A leader of sinners c. A deceptive follower	47 While he was still speaking a crowd came up, and the man who was called Judas, one of the Twelve, was leading them. He approached Jesus to kiss him, 48 But Jesus asked him, "Judas, are you betraying the Son of Man with a kiss?"	51 But Jesus answered, "No more of this!" And he touched the man's ear and healed him. 52 Then Jesus said to the chief priests, the officers of the temple guard, and the elders, who had come for him, "Am I leading a rebellion, that you have come with swords and clubs?	c. Jesus rebuked the disciples **3. Being blind to the Son of God: The religionists' sin**
2. Misunderstanding the Lord's will: The disciples' sin a. They asked if they should take up the sword	49 When Jesus' followers saw what was going to happen, they said, "Lord, should we strike with our swords?"	53 Every day I was with you in the temple courts, and you did not lay a hand on me. But this is your hour—when darkness reigns."	**4. Joining forces with the power of darkness: The people's sin**

DIVISION XI

THE SON OF MAN'S SUFFERINGS: HIS AGONY, TRIALS, AND CRUCIFIXION, 22:39–23:56

B. Jesus' Arrest: Terrible Sins Against Jesus, 22:47-53

(22:47-53) Introduction: it took only a few minutes to arrest Jesus. However, in those few minutes was painted a dramatic picture of four terrible sins against the Lord, sins that are repeated by too many in every generation.

1. Deserting Jesus: the betrayer's sin (vv.47-48).
2. Misunderstanding the Lord's will: the disciples' sin (vv.49 51).
3. Being blind to the Son of God: the religionists sin (v.52).
4. Joining forces with the power of darkness: the people's sin (v.53).

1 (22:47-48) **Unbelief—Desertion—Apostasy—Judas**: deserting the Lord, the sin committed by Judas the betrayer. Three things are seen in Judas' desertion.

1. He was a *professing* disciple, a man who claimed to be a follower of the Lord. In fact, he had actually been with the Lord and His followers for over two years. On this very evening, just a few hours before, he had been eating and fellowshipping with the Lord and the other disciples; but ever so quickly, he had turned away.

2. He was a *leader* of sinners, leading the world in its opposition to Jesus. Note the words "was leading them." As pointed out earlier, he chose the world before Jesus— the world's money, position, and recognition (fame). (See note—Mk.14:10.)

The crowd which Judas led is identified by Matthew and Mark as being arresting officers or temple police from the Sanhedrin. John says they included Roman soldiers. Matthew and Mark say they were armed. The soldiers, of course, had their swords; the elders and other officials of the High Priest had armed themselves with boards and sticks (see Mt.26:47).

3. He had a *deceptive* commitment to the Lord. Note what happened. It was dark. How would the temple guards be able to recognize Jesus in the dark and keep Him from slipping away? Judas thought and came up with a plan. He would identify Jesus for them by walking up and greeting Jesus with a kiss. A kiss was a sign of friendship and commitment among people in the East, in particular among

friends. Judas felt he could deceive the disciples; they would never suspect his sin.

What Judas planned, he did. The sin was bad, but the deception was worse. Jesus' question was searching: "Judas, are you betraying the Son of man with a kiss?" Note: the question was not a rebuke or reproach. Jesus was forcing Judas to think, to search his deceptive heart. He still wanted to reach Judas, if possible (see note—Mt.26:48-50).

Thought 1. How many profess Christ but do not really know Christ nor live for Christ? How many are deceivers just as Judas was: trying to make others think they are followers of Christ when they are really living *for themselves*? How many began to follow Christ but are now falling back into sin just as Judas did?

> **Friend deceives friend, and no one speaks the truth. They have taught their tongues to lie; they weary themselves with sinning. (Jer 9:5)**
> **The heart is deceitful above all things and beyond cure. Who can understand it? (Jer 17:9)**
> **Then we will no longer be infants, tossed back and forth by the waves, and blown here and there by every wind of teaching and by the cunning and craftiness of men in their deceitful scheming. (Eph 4:14)**
> **While evil men and impostors will go from bad to worse, deceiving and being deceived. (2 Tim 3:13)**
> **For there are many rebellious people, mere talkers and deceivers, especially those of the circumcision group. (Titus 1:10)**
> **See to it, brothers, that none of you has a sinful, unbelieving heart that turns away from the living God. (Heb 3:12)**
> **They will be paid back with harm for the harm they have done. Their idea of**

5

pleasure is to carouse in broad daylight. They are blots and blemishes, reveling in their pleasures while they feast with you. With eyes full of adultery, they never stop sinning; they seduce the unstable; they are experts in greed—an accursed brood! (2 Pet 2:13-14)

Many deceivers, who do not acknowledge Jesus Christ as coming in the flesh, have gone out into the world. Any such person is the deceiver and the antichrist. (2 John 1:7)

2 (22:49-51) **Flesh—Commitment—Carnal**: misunderstanding and ignoring the Lord's will, the sin committed by the disciples. Note two things.

1. The disciples misunderstood the Lord's will and the spiritual nature of His kingdom. They were ready to *war in the body or flesh*. The disciple referred to in v.50 was Peter, and the servant whose ear was cut off was Malchus (Jn.18:10). Jesus restored the ear, miraculously healed it (Lk.22:51).

Peter thought the Messiah's hour had come, that Jesus was now ready to free Israel and establish the throne of David as the dominant nation in the world (see notes—Mt.1:1; DEEPER STUDY # 2—1:18; DEEPER STUDY # 3—3:11; notes—11:1-6; 11:2-3; DEEPER STUDY # 1—11:5; DEEPER STUDY # 2—11:6; DEEPER STUDY # 1—12:16; notes—22:42; Lk.7:21-23). Peter drew his sword (note he had one) and struck, slashing off the ear of Malchus.

2. Jesus rebuked the disciples: their carnal commitment, their warring in the body or flesh.

⇒ He told Peter to put his sword back into its sheath where it belonged (Mt.26:52).
⇒ He healed Malchus' ear (Lk.22:51).

The picture painted by the disciples' behavior is carnal commitment, that is, acting and struggling in the flesh. The disciples took their stand for Jesus *in the flesh*. Therefore they failed, and eventually they deserted Jesus. Acting in the flesh will always result in failing and deserting Christ. The disciples' carnal commitment is seen in four mistakes. Each mistake is too often seen in the life of believers.

1. The disciples misunderstood the Lord's Word. First, they thought Jesus was to establish an earthly kingdom. They thought in terms of the earthly, the physical, the material. Therefore, they *failed to grasp the spiritual and eternal kingdom* proclaimed by Jesus. Second, they never accepted the Lord's Word. Jesus had predicted His death and forewarned the disciples, giving them extensive training for months (see notes—Mt.16:13-20; 16:21-28; 17:1-13; 17:22; 17:24-27). Yet they refused to give up their preconceived ideas to accept what Jesus was saying. Therefore, they did not see the eternal world of the Spirit nor the eternal salvation which Jesus was securing.

2. The disciples did not wait for instructions from Jesus. They acted on their own, took matters into their own hands. The disciples had asked, "Lord, should we strike with our swords?" But Jesus had not yet answered. However, this did not stop them; they went ahead and acted on their own.

Thought 1. How like so many of us! Too often, we act without waiting on the Lord.

3. The disciples did not ask Jesus what to do, not again and again. They did not *persist* until Jesus answered.

"Watch and pray so that you will not fall into temptation. The spirit is willing, but the body is weak." (Mat 26:41)

Be always on the watch, and pray that you may be able to escape all that is about to happen, and that you may be able to stand before the Son of Man." (Luke 21:36)

Look to the LORD and his strength; seek his face always. (1 Chr 16:11)

4. The disciples did not think clearly nor act wisely. Their actions could have led to the failure of God's will. It could have led to the death of many. That is what Jesus was saying: "Violence leads to violence. If you draw the sword, the soldiers will cut you down." Among God's people, the place of the sword is in the sheath, not drawn and slashing at people. God's people are to proclaim love and peace, not war and violence, not carnal and fleshly behavior.

So he said to me, "This is the word of the LORD to Zerubbabel: 'Not by might nor by power, but by my Spirit,' says the LORD Almighty. (Zec 4:6)

Those whom I love I rebuke and discipline. So be earnest, and repent. (Rev 3:19)

But in your hearts set apart Christ as Lord. Always be prepared to give an answer to everyone who asks you to give the reason for the hope that you have. But do this with gentleness and respect, (1 Pet 3:15)

3 (22:52) **Sin—Unbelief—Blindness**: being blind to the Son of God, the sin committed by the religionists. The religionists refused to accept Jesus as the Messiah (see note and DEEPER STUDY # 1—Mk.14:1-2). The question of Jesus was piercing. Why did the world treat Him as a thief? They acted as though He stole from them. He did not preach a message that allowed them to live as they wished; it was as though He took the right to live as they wished away from them. He did not praise them, boost their egos, honor their service and gifts. Rather, He told them they were lacking in discernment and sinful, dying and doomed if they did not repent and begin to live as God said (see note—Mt.26:55-56).

Thought 1. Note a crucial point so often not seen. Jesus had to tell the truth in order for men to be saved. God is love, but His love is not like a grandfather's indulgence that accepts wrongdoing. His love is the father's ache and acceptance of repentance and obedience. *Only through repentance and obedience can a man ever know the love of God* (see Jn.14:21, 23-24; 15:10, 14). God does not accept a man who does wrong and lives unrighteously. Jesus had to tell men the truth, for He could not deceive men. If men wanted to be acceptable to God and live in His love, then they had to turn away from sin and come to God, believing that He exists and diligently seeking Him.

And without faith it is impossible to please God, because anyone who comes to him must believe that he exists and that he rewards those who earnestly seek him. (Heb 11:6)

Whoever has my commands and obeys them, he is the one who loves me. He who loves me will be loved by my Father, and I too will love him and show myself to him." (John 14:21)

Jesus replied, "If anyone loves me, he will obey my teaching. My Father will love him, and we will come to him and make our home with him. He who does not love me will not obey my teaching. These words you hear are not my own; they belong to the Father who sent me. (John 14:23-24)

If you obey my commands, you will remain in my love, just as I have obeyed my Father's commands and remain in his love. You are my friends if you do what I command. (John 15:10, 14)

4 (22:53) **Satan**: joining forces with the power of darkness. What Jesus said was alarming: "This is your hour when darkness reigns." Those who opposed Jesus had joined forces with the power of darkness against Jesus. The power of darkness refers to the forces of evil, the evil one himself, Satan (Eph.6:12; Col.1:13). Note these points about the word "hour."

1. An hour is only a short time. It soon passes. Therefore, the power of darkness and those who oppose the Lord will last but a short time. Their hour will soon pass.

2. The power of darkness is always broken and conquered by light. When light appears, the presence and power of darkness are destroyed. So it is with God's Son, the Light of the world. The power of darkness and those who oppose Christ may have their hour now, but their hour is to end. He, the Light of the world, will arise and dispel the darkness and completely do away with it.

3. An hour soon passes, but then what is left? All the hours of life and of eternity. The power of darkness and those who oppose Christ may have an hour, but that will be all. However He, the Light of the world, will give Light to the world forever.

For our struggle is not against flesh and blood, but against the rulers, against the authorities, against the powers of this dark world and against the spiritual forces of evil in the heavenly realms. (Eph 6:12)

For he has rescued us from the dominion of darkness and brought us into the kingdom of the Son he loves, in whom we have redemption, the forgiveness of sins. (Col 1:13-14)

	C. Peter's Denial: The Great Tragedy of Denial, 22:54-62 (Mt.26:57, 69-75; Mk.14:53-54, 66-72; Jn.18:15-18, 25-27)	I don't know him," he said.	know Jesus
1. The cause of denial	54 Then seizing him, they led him away and took him into the house of the high priest. Peter followed at a distance.	58 A little later someone else saw him and said, "You also are one of them." "Man, I am not!" Peter replied.	**3. The denial of discipleship: Denying that one was a follower of Jesus**
a. Following at a distance: Not staying close to Jesus		59 About an hour later another asserted, "Certainly this fellow was with him, for he is a Galilean."	**4. The denial of ignorance: Claiming to know nothing about what was being said**
b. Sitting in the midst of a crowd: Mingling with the world	55 But when they had kindled a fire in the middle of the courtyard and had sat down together, Peter sat down with them.	60 Peter replied, "Man, I don't know what you're talking about!" Just as he was speaking, the rooster crowed.	a. The charge: Was a follower b. The emphatic denial: Knew nothing about Him
2. The denial of pretension: Pretending not to know Jesus	56 A servant girl saw him seated there in the firelight. She looked closely at him and said, "This man was with him."	61 The Lord turned and looked straight at Peter. Then Peter remembered the word the Lord had spoken to him: "Before the rooster crows today, you will disown me three times."	**5. The answer to denial** a. Remembering the Lord's word
a. The charge: Had been seen with Jesus			
b. The denial: Pretended not to	57 But he denied it. "Woman	62 And he went outside and wept bitterly.	b. Getting alone c. Sensing godly sorrow[DS1]

DIVISION XI

THE SON OF MAN'S SUFFERINGS: HIS AGONY, TRIALS, AND CRUCIFIXION, 22:39–23:56

C. Peter's Denial: The Great Tragedy of Denial, 22:54-62

(22:54-62) **Introduction**: denying Jesus is one of the greatest tragedies in all of life. Yet Jesus is denied often, not only by unbelievers but by believers as well. This passage is a study of denial, the awful tragedy of denying Jesus.

1. The cause of denial (vv.54-55).
2. The denial of pretension: pretending not to know Jesus (vv.56-57).
3. The denial of discipleship: denying that one was a follower of Jesus (v.58).
4. The denial of ignorance: claiming that one knows nothing about what is being said (vv.59-60).
5. The answer to denial (vv.61-62).

1 (22:54-55) **Apostasy—Jesus Christ, Denied**: the cause of denial given in these verses is twofold. Peter failed Jesus and failed Him miserably.

1. "Peter followed at a distance." *Following Jesus at a distance* means not walking close to Him, not standing and being identified with Him. A man who follows at a distance is not focusing on Christ. His mind and life are not fixed upon the Lord. His commitment is weak; therefore, he is easily...

- distracted by the world and drawn into its ways.
- stricken with fear—the fear of ridicule, embarrassment, abuse, persecution, being cut off, shunned, ignored, ostracized.

> **For God did not give us a spirit of timidity, but a spirit of power, of love and of self-discipline. So do not be ashamed to testify about our Lord, or ashamed of me his prisoner. But join with me in suffering for the gospel, by the power of God, (2 Tim 1:7-8)**

2. Peter "sat down with them" [the crowd], the crowd which represented the world of rejecters. Very frankly, Peter was failing Jesus miserably. Sitting down among the crowd was the last place he should have been. He, of course, should have never forsaken Jesus. But having fled, he should have been off alone with God in prayer, seeking answers and understanding from God (see notes—Mt.26:51-52; 26:55-56). Or he should have been with the other apostles, leading them to seek the face of God for understanding and direction.

> **"Therefore come out from them and be separate, says the Lord. Touch no unclean thing, and I will receive you." "I will be a Father to you, and you will be my sons and daughters, says the Lord Almighty." (2 Cor 6:17-18)**

2 (22:56-57) **Apostasy—Jesus Christ, Denied**: the denial of pretension—pretending not to know Jesus. When confronted, this denial says, "I have nothing to do with Christ."

Note what happened. A maid "looked closely" at Peter. She stared at him, observed him closely, thinking she had seen him with Jesus. She concluded that Peter was one of the Lord's followers: "This man was with Him." There seems to be no threat or danger in this statement to Peter. At worst it seems that it would have led only to some bantering and ridicule. The rejecters standing around were naturally bantering back and forth about Jesus and His claims, considering Him to have been a fool. Peter had an opportunity, perhaps, to be a witness for Jesus, humbly sharing about the love and enormous care of Jesus for people. Perhaps he could have helped to turn some who were standing there to Jesus, or at least stopped some of the mob's ridiculing. We must always remember that John was somewhere in the palace as well, and as far as we know, he was maintaining his composure and testimony for Jesus.

Peter cracked under his fear. He denied Jesus, pretending he did not know Him or have anything to do with Him.

Thought 1. Weak believers fear the crowd. When in church they readily profess Christ, but out in the world, at work or at school, they fear being known as believers. They pretend not to know Christ.

> But whoever disowns me before men, I will disown him before my Father in heaven. (Mat 10:33)
> A false witness will not go unpunished, and he who pours out lies will not go free. (Prov 19:5)
> But in your hearts set apart Christ as Lord. Always be prepared to give an answer to everyone who asks you to give the reason for the hope that you have. But do this with gentleness and respect, (1 Pet 3:15)

3 (22:58) **Apostasy—Jesus Christ, Denied**: the denial of discipleship—denying that one is a follower of Jesus. When confronted, this denial is more emphatic and vocal, "I am not a disciple, not a follower of Christ."

Note the charge: "You are also one of them." The charge was true.
- ⇒ Peter had been with Jesus. He was an apostle; in fact, he was the leader of the apostles.
- ⇒ Peter was the disciple who had professed that Jesus was the Christ, the Son of God (Mt.16:16).
- ⇒ Peter was the disciple who had sworn loyalty to Jesus even if it meant death (Mt.26:33-35).

Peter emphatically denied that he was a disciple, a follower of Jesus: "I am not!" Peter was falling (progressing) more and more into sin. He was denying Jesus because he was not by His side, but *standing among* the Lord's rejecters.
- ⇒ He was standing among the Lord's rejecters because he had fled the Lord.
- ⇒ He had fled the Lord because he had acted in the flesh (see note—Lk.22:49-51).
- ⇒ He had acted in the flesh because he had not accepted the Lord's words for what they said.

> If anyone is ashamed of me and my words in this adulterous and sinful generation, the Son of Man will be ashamed of him when he comes in his Father's glory with the holy angels." (Mark 8:38)
> So do not be ashamed to testify about our Lord, or ashamed of me his prisoner. But join with me in suffering for the gospel, by the power of God, (2 Tim 1:8)
> Be strong and courageous. Do not be afraid or terrified because of them, for the LORD your God goes with you; he will never leave you nor forsake you." (Deu 31:6)

4 (22:59-60) **Apostasy—Jesus Christ, Denied**: the denial of ignorance—claiming that one knows nothing about what is being said. This is the denial that claims ignorance, "I do not know what you are talking about; I know absolutely nothing about the matter." Matthew and Mark say Peter began to curse and swear, *denying any knowledge whatsoever about Jesus.*

Note: this accuser is sure Peter was a follower of Jesus. The man "was certain," insisted upon the fact. He even identified Peter's nationality, a Galilean Jew. It was common knowledge that Jesus' disciples were Galileans.

Peter's chest was bound to be pounding with emotion and fear. His thoughts were flying, trying to figure how to escape. His emotions just burst forth in cursing and swearing, a forceful denial: "Man, I don't know what you're talking about." Note that this denial occurred about one hour after the last one. Peter's failure was a deteriorating failure.
- ⇒ At first, he pretended not to know Jesus.
- ⇒ Then he fell even farther. He emphatically denied being a disciple.
- ⇒ Now, he claimed total ignorance of all. He cursed and swore that he knew absolutely nothing about Jesus.

This is the point: Peter stayed in the crowd, still stood around the rejecters of Jesus—even after they had led him to deny Jesus twice. He was trying to be *of the world*, one of the crowd, when he should have been off praying and seeking to understand the ways of God.

> Do not set foot on the path of the wicked or walk in the way of evil men. (Prov 4:14)
> Therefore, dear friends, since you already know this, be on your guard so that you may not be carried away by the error of lawless men and fall from your secure position. (2 Pet 3:17)
> They claim to know God, but by their actions they deny him. They are detestable, disobedient and unfit for doing anything good. (Titus 1:16)
> If we endure, we will also reign with him. If we disown him, he will also disown us; (2 Tim 2:12)
> Without being frightened in any way by those who oppose you. This is a sign to them that they will be destroyed, but that you will be saved—and that by God. (Phil 1:28)
> With many other words he warned them; and he pleaded with them, "Save yourselves from this corrupt generation." (Acts 2:40)

5 (22:60-62) **Repentance—Confession**: three steps were involved in Peter's repentance.

1. Remembering the Lord's words. Apparently while the rooster was crowing, the Lord, standing in the chamber of the palace, turned around and caught the eye of Peter (Lk.22:61). And Peter, eye to eye with the Lord, remembered the words the Lord had spoken to him:

> "Simon, Simon, Satan has asked to sift you as wheat. But I have prayed for you, Simon, that your faith may not fail. And when you have turned back, strengthen your brothers." (Luke 22:31-32)

In the midst of all His own pain and suffering, the Lord's look told Peter that His Lord had not forgotten him. The Lord still loved and cared for Him and wanted his loyalty and service. Jesus had prayed for Peter, and the power of that prayer was now moving in Peter's heart and life. Peter now remembered His Lord's word and that word began to take effect.

2. Getting alone. Peter left as fast as he safely could from the porch or courtyard through the gate out into the night to get alone at last with God. He was broken, full of anguish and pain for having failed his Lord: he "wept bitterly."

3. Expressing godly sorrow: repentance (see DEEPER STUDY # 1—2 Cor.7:10).

If we confess our sins, he is faithful and just and will forgive us our sins and purify us from all unrighteousness. (1 John 1:9)

Repent of this wickedness and pray to the Lord. Perhaps he will forgive you for having such a thought in your heart. (Acts 8:22)

And prayed: "O my God, I am too ashamed and disgraced to lift up my face to you, my God, because our sins are higher than our heads and our guilt has reached to the heavens. (Ezra 9:6)

Now make confession to the LORD, the God of your fathers, and do his will. Separate yourselves from the peoples around you and from your foreign wives." (Ezra 10:11)

My guilt has overwhelmed me like a burden too heavy to bear. (Psa 38:4)

For I know my transgressions, and my sin is always before me. (Psa 51:3)

When my heart was grieved and my spirit embittered, (Psa 73:21;see John 16:8)

He who conceals his sins does not prosper, but whoever confesses and renounces them finds mercy. (Prov 28:13)

Only acknowledge your guilt— you have rebelled against the LORD your God, you have scattered your favors to foreign gods under every spreading tree, and have not obeyed me,'" declares the LORD. (Jer 3:13)

DEEPER STUDY # 1
(22:62) **Repentance**: see note and DEEPER STUDY # 1—Acts 17:29-30.

1. The attitude of religion & the world toward the claims of Jesus	D. Jesus Tried Before the Sanhedrin Court: The Phenomenal Claims of Jesus, 22:63-71 (Mt.26:57-68; 27:1; Mk.14:53-65; 15:1; Jn.18:12-14, 19-24)	of the law, met together, and Jesus was led before them. 67 "If you are the Christ," they said, "tell us." Jesus answered, "If I tell you, you will not believe me, 68 And if I asked you, you would not answer.	2. The first claim: He is the Messiah
a. There was physical & verbal abuse	63 The men who were guarding Jesus began mocking and beating him. 64 They blindfolded him and demanded, "Prophesy! Who hit you?" 65 And they said many other insulting things to him.	69 But from now on, the Son of Man will be seated at the right hand of the mighty God." 70 They all asked, "Are you then the Son of God?" He replied, "You are right in saying I am."	3. The second claim: He is the Son of Man—who will be exalted to the right hand of God
			4. The third claim: He is the Son of God
b. There was legal abuse—a formal trial[DS1]	66 At daybreak the council of the elders of the people, both the chief priests and teachers	71 Then they said, "Why do we need any more testimony? We have heard it from his own lips."	5. The conclusion: The claims were understood but rejected

DIVISION XI

THE SON OF MAN'S SUFFERINGS: HIS AGONY, TRIALS, AND CRUCIFIXION, 22:39–23:56

D. Jesus Tried Before the Sanhedrin Court: The Phenomenal Claims of Jesus, 22:63-71

(22:63-71) **Introduction**: this is the first trial of Jesus covered by Luke. The thrust of the trial was the phenomenal claims of Jesus, claims which demand a decision from every man.

1. The attitude of religion and the world toward Jesus' claims (vv.63-66).
2. The first claim: He is the Messiah (vv.67-68).
3. The second claim: He is the Son of Man—who will be exalted to the right hand of God (v.69).
4. The third claim: He is the Son of God (v.70).
5. Conclusion: the claims were understood, but rejected (v.71).

1 (22:63-66) **World, Response to Jesus—Persecution, of Jesus Christ—Jesus Christ, Trials of**: the attitude of religion and the world to Jesus' claims. The world and formal religion opposed Jesus. This is clearly seen in the treatment of Jesus during the night while He was being held for trial the next morning.

1. There was (and is today) physical and verbal abuse. They ridiculed and mocked and shamed and beat Him. Why? Because of His claims.

> **Remember the words I spoke to you: 'No servant is greater than his master.' If they persecuted me, they will persecute you also. If they obeyed my teaching, they will obey yours also. (John 15:20. Also refer to Jn.15:20-25.)**

2. There was ridicule of His spiritual power. If He were the Son of God, He should know all things, so they mocked and challenged His power: "Prophesy! who hit you?" But God gives no signs, not to the mocking and obstinate and devilish unbeliever. (See note—Mk.8:12.)

3. There were all kinds of blasphemy and cursing spoken against Him. (How tragic! Yet, how much like men today!)

Note the setting for the formal trial of Jesus. This was a trial by the Sanhedrin, the ruling body of the Jews which included both religious and lay leaders (see DEEPER STUDY # 1, *Sanhedrin*—Mt.26:59). Jesus stood before them all on trial for His life. Note the words "met together": they gathered, resorted, *flocked together* just as a body of vultures over their prey. There is also the idea of accompanying. The picture is that of the Jewish leaders flocking or herding together around Jesus, of being called to accompany one another to their respective seats, ready to pounce on Jesus. There is no question about the evil of their hearts. They *were* ready to pounce on and eliminate Him.

The court was stacked against Jesus. The leaders, both lay and religious, had already *determined* to reject and oppose Him. He was a threat to both their nation and their personal security and position. They feared the loss of both, so they were set on killing Him. (For a discussion of the reasons for their opposition, see notes—Mt.12:1-8; note and DEEPER STUDY # 1—12:10; note—15:1-20; DEEPER STUDY # 2—15:6-9; DEEPER STUDY # 3—16:12.)

Thought 1. The religionists rejected and opposed Christ for two primary reasons, the same two reasons that men reject and oppose Him today.

1) Men are unwilling to deny self, to surrender all they are and have to Christ. They fear the loss of some-thing—some security, money, position, power, or pleasure. They love the world and self more than they are willing to love God.
2) Men are unwilling to deny their institutional religion: their religious practices that are *man-made*, *man-conceived*, *man-honoring*.

Thought 2. Men do *flock together* to oppose Christ. It is easier to oppose Him in the presence of others.

> **Dear friend, do not imitate what is evil but what is good. Anyone who does what is good is from God. Anyone who does what is evil has not seen God. (3 John 1:11)**
> **Anyone, then, who knows the good he ought to do and doesn't do it, sins. (James 4:17)**

11

DEEPER STUDY # 1

(22:66-71) **Jesus, Trials of**: there were at least six trials.

1. An informal trial during the night before Annas (Jn.18:12-14, 19-23).

2. An informal trial by night before Caiaphas and some Sanhedrin officials to find a charge against Jesus (Mt.26:57-68; Mk.14:53-65; Lk.22:54, 63-65).

3. An early morning formal trial before a quickly assembled Sanhedrin to secure the verdict of the full Sanhedrin and to formulate the charge against Jesus (Mt.27:1; Mk.15:1; Lk.22:66-71).

4. A preliminary questioning by Pilate (Mt.27:2, 11-14; Mk.15:1-5; Lk.23:1-5; Jn.18:28-38).

5. A preliminary questioning by Herod (Lk.23:6-12).

6. The formal Roman trial before Pilate (Mt.27:15-26; Mk.15:6-15; Lk.23:13-25; Jn.18:39-40).

The other events following Jesus' arrest seem to be:

1. Peter's denial (Mt.26:58, 69-75; Mk.14:54, 66-72; Lk.22:54-62; Jn.18:15-18, 25-27).

2. Judas' suicide (Mt.27:3-10; Acts 1:18-19). Both of these events took place between the first and second trial.

3. Jesus crowned with thorns and severely beaten by the Roman soldiers (Mt.27:27-30; Mk.15:16-19; Jn.19:1-3).

4. Simon's carrying Jesus' cross (Mt.27:31-32; Mk.15:20-21; Lk.23:26).

5. Jesus warning the women of the coming judgment upon Jerusalem (Lk.23:27-31). (See note—Mt.26:57; 26:59.)

2 (22:67-68) **Jesus Christ, Claims**: Jesus claimed to be the Messiah. The council did not come right out and accuse Jesus. They wanted Him to incriminate Himself; therefore, they questioned Him: "If you are the Christ [Messiah]... Tell us." But Jesus could not answer, not directly. Note two facts.

1. They did not understand the true Messiahship of God. God's Messiahship is spiritual and eternal, not physical and material (see note—Eph.1:3). Jesus had come to save men spiritually, not materially. Therefore if He told them, they would not believe me; and if He asked them questions which would lead them to the truth, they would not answer. He had done this often (Lk.20:7, 26, 40).

2. Jesus did not deny His Messiahship. The way He answered the council was an affirmation. Note His exact words, "If I tell you, you will not believe me." It was as though He said, "I am, but if I tell you, declare it vocally, you will not believe it." (See notes—Mt.1:1; DEEPER STUDY # 2—1:18; note—Lk.19:36-38 see Mk.11:1-11 for concepts of Messiah.)

> The woman said, "I know that Messiah" (called Christ) "is coming. When he comes, he will explain everything to us." Then Jesus declared, "I who speak to you am he." (John 4:25-26)
>
> So Jesus said, "When you have lifted up the Son of Man, then you will know that I am the one I claim to be and that I do nothing on my own but speak just what the Father has taught me. The one who sent me is with me; he has not left me alone, for I always do what pleases him." (John 8:28-29)

3 (22:69) **Jesus Christ, Claims**: Jesus claimed to be the Son of Man who will be exalted. Jesus was really making three claims.

1. That He is the Son of Man (see notes—Lk.4:20-21; Jn.1:51; DEEPER STUDY # 3—Mt.8:20. See Dan.7:13-14.)

2. That He will not remain dead even if they kill Him. He will be raised into God's presence.

3. That He will be exalted to sit on the right hand of the power of God.

> And who through the Spirit of holiness was declared with power to be the Son of God by his resurrection from the dead: Jesus Christ our Lord. (Rom 1:4)
>
> God has raised this Jesus to life, and we are all witnesses of the fact. Exalted to the right hand of God, he has received from the Father the promised Holy Spirit and has poured out what you now see and hear. For David did not ascend to heaven, and yet he said, "'The Lord said to my Lord: "Sit at my right hand until I make your enemies a footstool for your feet."' "Therefore let all Israel be assured of this: God has made this Jesus, whom you crucified, both Lord and Christ." (Acts 2:32-36)
>
> And his incomparably great power for us who believe. That power is like the working of his mighty strength, which he exerted in Christ when he raised him from the dead and seated him at his right hand in the heavenly realms, far above all rule and authority, power and dominion, and every title that can be given, not only in the present age but also in the one to come. (Eph 1:19-21)
>
> Therefore God exalted him to the highest place and gave him the name that is above every name, that at the name of Jesus every knee should bow, in heaven and on earth and under the earth, and every tongue confess that Jesus Christ is Lord, to the glory of God the Father. (Phil 2:9-11)

4 (22:70) **Jesus Christ, Claims**: Jesus claimed to be the Son of God. Note several facts.

1. "They all" now questioned Jesus. The picture is that of an uproar, voices reacting to His claim to be the Son of Man, voices bursting forth together shouting: "Are you then the Son of God?"

2. The definite article "the" is important. They were not asking if He were *a* son of God like many men claim. They asked if He was "the Son of God."

3. Jesus unquestionably claimed to be "the Son of God." (See note—Mk.14:62 for more discussion.)

> Then those who were in the boat worshiped him, saying, "Truly you are the Son of God." (Mat 14:33)
>
> The beginning of the gospel about Jesus Christ, the Son of God. (Mark 1:1)
>
> I have seen and I testify that this is the Son of God." (John 1:34)
>
> "For God so loved the world that he gave his one and only Son, that whoever believes in him shall not perish but have eternal life. For God did not send his Son into the world to condemn the world, but to save the world through him. Whoever believes in him is not condemned, but who

ever does not believe stands condemned already because he has not believed in the name of God's one and only Son. (John 3:16-18)

Jesus heard that they had thrown him out, and when he found him, he said, "Do you believe in the Son of Man?" "Who is he, sir?" the man asked. "Tell me so that I may believe in him." Jesus said, "You have now seen him; in fact, he is the one speaking with you." (John 9:35-37)

What about the one whom the Father set apart as his very own and sent into the world? Why then do you accuse me of blasphemy because I said, 'I am God's Son'? (John 10:36)

Jesus said to her, "I am the resurrection and the life. He who believes in me will live, even though he dies; and whoever lives and believes in me will never die. Do you believe this?" "Yes, Lord," she told him, "I believe that you are the Christ, the Son of God, who was to come into the world." (John 11:25-27)

How much more severely do you think a man deserves to be punished who has trampled the Son of God under foot, who has treated as an unholy thing the blood of the covenant that sanctified him, and who has insulted the Spirit of grace? (Heb 10:29)

If anyone acknowledges that Jesus is the Son of God, God lives in him and he in God. (1 John 4:15)

5 (22:71) **Jesus Christ, Claims**: the claim of Jesus was understood, but the leaders rejected His claim. Jesus had both accepted and claimed the charge being made against Him. He was...
- The Messiah.
- The Son of God.
- The Son of Man.

They had heard enough. In their obstinate unbelief, they condemned Him to death—condemned the Man who had come to save the world from its terrible plight of sin and death, from its desperate need for health and love and for salvation and life.

Just as the Son of Man did not come to be served, but to serve, and to give his life as a ransom for many." (Mat 20:28)

For the Son of Man came to seek and to save what was lost." (Luke 19:10)

	CHAPTER 23 **E. Jesus' First Trial Before Pilate & Herod: The Shirking of Duty & Personal Concern, 23:1-12** (Mt.27:11-14; Mk.15:1-5; Jn.18:28-38)	6 On hearing this, Pilate asked if the man was a Galilean.
1. The setting: The Sanhedrin dragged Jesus before Pilate[DS1]	Then the whole assembly rose and led him off to Pilate.	7 When he learned that Jesus was under Herod's jurisdiction, he sent him to Herod, who was also in Jerusalem at that time.
2. The trial before Pilate: Shirking duty	2 And they began to accuse him, saying, "We have found this man subverting our nation. He opposes payment of taxes to Caesar and claims to be Christ, a king."	8 When Herod saw Jesus, he was greatly pleased, because for a long time he had been wanting to see him. From what he had heard about him, he hoped to see him perform some miracle.

a. The charges against Jesus[DS2]
  1) He is a revolutionary
  2) He opposes taxes
  3) He claims to be a King		

b. The questioning of Pilate & the claim of Jesus	3 So Pilate asked Jesus, "Are you the king of the Jews?" "Yes, it is as you say," Jesus replied.	9 He plied him with many questions, but Jesus gave him no answer.
c. The verdict by Pilate: Jesus was innocent	4 Then Pilate announced to the chief priests and the crowd, "I find no basis for a charge against this man."	10 The chief priests and the teachers of the law were standing there, vehemently accusing him.
d. The bitter protest & enlarged charge of the crowd	5 But they insisted, "He stirs up the people all over Judea by his teaching. He started in Galilee and has come all the way here."	11 Then Herod and his soldiers ridiculed and mocked him. Dressing him in an elegant robe, they sent him back to Pilate. 12 That day Herod and Pilate became friends—before this they had been enemies.

e. The attempt by Pilate to escape his duty	
3. The questioning before Herod: Shirking concern	
a. He sought the spectacular	
b. He was the only man Jesus never answered	
c. He listened to false charges by the religionists	
d. He did not take Jesus seriously: Ridiculed & mocked Him—contemptuously	
4. The conclusion: Pilate & Herod were brought together in their opposition to Jesus	

DIVISION XI

THE SON OF MAN'S SUFFERINGS: HIS AGONY, TRIALS, AND CRUCIFIXION, 22:39–23:56

E. Jesus' First Trial Before Pilate and Herod: The Shirking of Duty and Personal Concern, 23:1-12

(23:1-12) **Introduction**: this passage is a clear portrait of two men who shirked duty and personal concern.

1. The setting: the Sanhedrin dragged Jesus before Pilate (v.1).
2. The trial before Pilate: shirking duty (vv.2-7).
3. The questioning before Herod: shirking concern (vv.8-11).
4. The conclusion: Pilate and Herod were brought together in their opposition to Jesus (v.12).

1 (23:1) **Religionists**: the Sanhedrin dragged Jesus to Pilate. Feelings ran deep. The depth of their obstinate unbelief is seen in the fact that "the *whole assembly* rose and led Him off to Pilate." Just picture the scene. All members present (seventy one when a full body was present) marched Him to Pilate. They were so opposed to Him that they wanted the full weight of their position and their comrades standing against Him.

> **Thought 1.** Observe obstinate unbelievers. They try to convince and secure as much support as possible against Christ and His followers. Why? To protect their worldly desires and security, their position and authority and wealth.

DEEPER STUDY # 1
(23:1-7) **Pilate**: see DEEPER STUDY # 1—Lk.23:13.

2 (23:2-7) **Jesus Christ, Trials—Pilate**: the trial before Pilate, a picture of *shirking duty*. Note five points.

1. The political charges against Jesus were three (see DEEPER STUDY # 2—Lk.23:2).
2. The questioning of Pilate and the claim of Jesus. This was one of the charges brought against Jesus, and in the eyes of Rome it would be the most serious. Pilate, somewhat surprised by the charge, scornfully asked Jesus, "Are you the King of the Jews?" Jesus strongly claimed that He was: "Yes, it is as you say." However, as John points out, Jesus clearly stated that His kingdom was not of this world. His kingdom was spiritual (Jn.18:36-37).

> **Thought 1.** Jesus is not a political revolutionary, not a threat to any civil government. He is the King of man's spirit and of heaven, of the spiritual dimension of being, not of earth. He came to rule and reign in the hearts and lives of men, in the realm of the spiritual and eternal, not in the realm of the physical and temporal (see note—Eph.1:3).

3. The verdict of Pilate: Jesus was innocent. Note: this is a public verdict. Pilate actually pronounced Jesus innocent to the leaders and the people. However, as shall be seen and as is the case with so many, he lacked the *inner strength* to stand by his convictions. He gave in to the world, going along with their wish.

4. The bitter protest and enlarged charge. The unbelievers, fitfully aroused, accused Jesus. They were close-minded: obstinate, bitter, spiteful. They said He was guilty of leading a revolution throughout all Israel, from Galilee to Jerusalem.

It should be noted that Jesus' purpose was not to defend Himself nor to escape death. His purpose was to surrender to the *sinful behavior* of men. The *sinful behavior* to which He submitted was...

- the very depth of sin itself.
- the ultimate demonstration of sin.
- the greatest sin that could be committed.

The act of sin to which He subjected Himself was the rejection and killing of the Son of God. Standing there before His accusers, He said nothing, enduring their awful indignities. He endured because He was purposed to die for the sins of men.

Note that Pilate actually declared Jesus innocent four different times (Lk.23:4, 14, 15, 22; see Jn.18:38; 19:4, 6).

5. The attempt to escape one's duty (Pilate). Pilate wished to release Jesus, for he knew the Lord was innocent. However, he had to guard against upsetting the leaders of the Jewish nation. He was in a dilemma. When he heard Galilee mentioned, he saw a way out of his dilemma. Herod, who was ruler of Galilee, was in town for the Passover. He could send Jesus over to Herod and let him pass judgment. As a Galilean, Jesus belonged under the jurisdiction of Herod.

The point to note is this: Pilate lacked the courage to do what was right. He knew Jesus was innocent, yet he sought to *escape his duty* to declare the truth. He made four attempts to shirk his duty. (1) He tried to get the Jews to handle the matter themselves (Lk.18:31). (2) He sent Jesus to Herod (Lk.23:7). (3) He tried to get the Jews to accept Jesus as the prisoner to be released at the Passover (Lk.23:17-19; Mk.15:6). (4) He suggested flogging Jesus and then letting Him go (Lk.23:16).

> **Thought 1.** A man who seeks to escape his duty is an unworthy leader. He is not worthy of the responsibility (position, call, or duty).

> **He is a double-minded man, unstable in all he does. (James 1:8)**
>
> **Come near to God and he will come near to you. Wash your hands, you sinners, and purify your hearts, you double-minded. (James 4:8)**
>
> **"No servant can serve two masters. Either he will hate the one and love the other, or he will be devoted to the one and despise the other. You cannot serve both God and Money." (Luke 16:13)**
>
> **Their heart is deceitful, and now they must bear their guilt. The LORD will demolish their altars and destroy their sacred stones. (Hosea 10:2)**

DEEPER STUDY # 2

(23:2) **Jesus Christ, Charges Against**: three political charges were leveled against Jesus.

1. He was charged with perverting the nation, that is, of treason, of being a revolutionary and committing sedition against Rome. The charge, of course, was false. Jesus was not out to pervert people from an earthly nation; He was out to convert people to a heavenly world, to God and His kingdom which were not of this earth (Jn.19:36).

2. He was charged with disobeying the laws of the nation, in particular for not paying taxes. Of course this charge was also false. Jesus had taught that obedience to earthly government was absolutely essential for the believer. (See outline and notes—Lk.20:19-26.)

3. He was charged with claiming to be King, with being a rival to Caesar. Again, this charge was false.

   a. The very reason the Jewish leaders were not accepting Him (so they claimed) was because He had come in the meekness and love of God, not in the armed might of God, liberating their nation from the Roman conquerors (see DEEPER STUDY # 2—Mt.1:18).

   b. Jesus had actually refused to let the people set Him up as King (Jn.6:15).

---

3 (23:8-11) **Herod's Hardened Heart**: the questioning before Herod, a picture of shirking personal concern. Herod showed no concern whatsoever for the truth, nor for his own soul. The possibility that the true Messiah might actually be standing before Him never crossed his mind. (See note, pt.3—Lk.3:1. Also see DEEPER STUDY # 1, 2, *Herod*—Mt.14:1-14 for more discussion.)

1. Herod sought only the spectacular. He had heard many things about Jesus, the amazing power and miracles He had manifested. As a ruler, a very special person, Herod wanted and felt he deserved...

- the privilege of some sign
- the privilege of gazing
- the privilege of some spectacle

Jesus' power, of course, was not to be used for the spectacular, not for the purpose of satisfying an unbeliever's curiosity. (See notes—Lk.4:9-12; 11:20 for more discussion.)

2. Herod was the only man Jesus never answered. Herod's own household had been penetrated with the gospel. Chuza, Herod's personal steward (Lk.8:3), and Manaen, Herod's foster brother (Acts 13:1), were believers. The nobleman or court official mentioned in the story shared by Jesus was also probably of Herod's court (Jn.4:46). Apparently, the gospel as lived by these persons had little effect upon Herod. Their sharing was but religious foolishness to him. He treated their reports with disdain, perhaps with some abuse. Jesus, knowing the hopelessness of his unresponsive heart, wasted no time and no words upon him. Jesus said nothing to him at all.

3. Herod listened to false charges by the religionists. He had failed to listen to John the Baptist (Lk.9:7-9) and to the witnesses in his own household. He had heard many things about Christ (v.8), yet he had refused to listen, to truly hear and heed. But now, with Jesus standing before him, he listened to the false charges of those who opposed Jesus.

4. Herod set Jesus at naught, treated Him as unimportant. The word "ridicule" (exouthenesas) means to count as nothing, to make nothing of, to think something is unimportant, to count as zero—therefore, to treat with utter contempt.

Note the contrast in the verse. Herod sat there as King with his soldiers surrounding him, and Jesus stood there beaten and battered in torn, ragged clothes. Herod, judging by appearance, counted the Man who claimed to be the Son of God as nothing. This Man and His claim did not matter, not to Herod.

Thought 1. Many count Christ as unimportant. They think He does not matter—that He can be excluded from life, that He and His claim are meaningless. Such people go about counting their own lives and worldly ways dear unto themselves. (see Lk.9:24; 17:33.)

Whoever tries to keep his life will lose it, and whoever loses his life will preserve it. (Luke 17:33)

"Be careful, or your hearts will be weighed down with dissipation, drunkenness and the anxieties of life, and that day will close on you unexpectedly like a trap. (Luke 21:34)

Whoever believes in the Son has eternal life, but whoever rejects the Son will not see life, for God's wrath remains on him." (John 3:36)

I told you that you would die in your sins; if you do not believe that I am the one I claim to be, you will indeed die in your sins." (John 8:24)

See to it, brothers, that none of you has a sinful, unbelieving heart that turns away from the living God. (Heb 3:12)

4 (23:12) **World, Rejection of Jesus**: Pilate and Herod became friends; the worldly are brought together in their opposition against Christ.

1. Pilate tried selfishly to protect himself[DS1]	F. Jesus' Second Trial Before Pilate: The Tragedy of a Compromising Man, 23:13-25 (Mt.27:15-25; Mk.15:6-15; Jn.18:39-19:16) 13 Pilate called together the chief priests, the rulers and the people,	19 (Barabbas had been thrown into prison for an insurrection in the city, and for murder.) 20 Wanting to release Jesus, Pilate appealed to them again.	3. Pilate gave in to worldly pressure
a. A man who knew the truth	14 And said to them, "You brought me this man as one who was inciting the people to rebellion. I have examined him in your presence and have found no basis for your charges against him. 15 Neither has Herod, for he sent him back to us; as you can see, he has done nothing to deserve death.	21 But they kept shouting, "Crucify him! Crucify him!" 22 For the third time he spoke to them: "Why? What crime has this man committed? I have found in him no grounds for the death penalty. Therefore I will have him punished and then release him."	a. He knew the truth: Jesus was innocent
b. A man who tried to appease others out of fear 2. Pilate tried to compromise truth & clear evidence	16 Therefore, I will punish him and then release him."[17] 18 With one voice they cried out, "Away with this man! Release Barabbas to us!"	23 But with loud shouts they insistently demanded that he be crucified, and their shouts prevailed. 24 So Pilate decided to grant their demand. 25 He released the man who had been thrown into prison for insurrection and murder, the one they asked for, and surrendered Jesus to their will.	b. He faced loud voices against Jesus c. He compromised: Gave in to the worldly cries d. He allowed injustice, wrong, & evil to be done

DIVISION XI

THE SON OF MAN'S SUFFERINGS: HIS AGONY, TRIALS, AND CRUCIFIXION, 22:39–23:56

F. Jesus' Second Trial Before Pilate: The Tragedy of a Compromising Man, 23:13-25

(23:13-25) **Introduction**: compromising with the world is sin. Compromise always leads to trouble and tragedy. Pilate is the picture of a man whose compromise led to the greatest tragedy in human history.

1. Pilate tried selfishly to protect himself (vv.13-16).
2. Pilate tried to compromise truth and clear evidence (vv.17-21).
3. Pilate gave in to worldly pressure (vv.22-25).

1 (23:13-16) **Compromise—Appeasement—Injustice**: Pilate tried selfishly to protect himself. He called the court back into session. A decision had been made; he was now ready to give his verdict.

⇒ He had examined Jesus and found no fault in Him: Jesus was innocent.
⇒ He had sent Jesus to Herod for a verdict, and Herod found Jesus innocent.
⇒ No crime worthy of death had been committed by Jesus. Pilate had decided, therefore, that he would chastise Jesus and release Him.

Note that Pilate was trying to appease the Jews. He knew the truth: Jesus was innocent. Jesus should be released and the Jews' behavior rebuked, but Pilate feared displeasing and inflaming the Jews. He was afraid they might cause trouble for him, reporting him to Rome and causing him to lose his position and rule (see DEEPER STUDY # 1—Lk.23:13). Throughout the whole scene Pilate's primary interest was himself, not truth and justice.

Thought 1. A compromising man is self-centered. He seeks to protect himself even at the expense of the truth and justice. He fears losing…
• position, power, influence
• job security, image, acceptance, friends

"'Do not pervert justice; do not show partiality to the poor or favoritism to the great, but judge your neighbor fairly. (Lev 19:15)

"How long will you defend the unjust and show partiality to the wicked? Selah (Psa 82:2)

And I saw something else under the sun: In the place of judgment—wickedness was there, in the place of justice—wickedness was there. (Eccl 3:16)

"So I have caused you to be despised and humiliated before all the people, because you have not followed my ways but have shown partiality in matters of the law." (Mal 2:9)

I charge you, in the sight of God and Christ Jesus and the elect angels, to keep these instructions without partiality, and to do nothing out of favoritism. (1 Tim 5:21)

This day I call heaven and earth as witnesses against you that I have set before you life and death, blessings and curses. Now choose life, so that you and your children may live (Deu 30:19)

DEEPER STUDY # 1

(23:13) **Pilate**: the procurator of Judea. He was directly responsible to the Emperor for the administrative and financial management of the country. A man had to work himself up through the political and military ranks to become a procurator. Pilate was, therefore, an able man, experienced in the affairs of politics and government as well as the military. He held office for ten years which shows that he was highly trusted by the Roman government. However, the Jews despised Pilate, and Pilate despised the Jews for their intense practice of religion. When Pilate became procurator of Judea, he did two things that aroused the people's bitter hatred against him forever. First, on his state visits to Jerusalem, he and his military guard rode their stallions into the city with the Roman standard, an eagle sitting atop a pole. All previous governors had removed the standard because of the Jews' opposition to idols. Second, Pilate launched the construction of a new water supply for Jerusalem. To finance the project, he took the money out of the temple treasury. The Jews never forgot or forgave this act. They bitterly opposed Pilate all through his reign, and he treated them with equal contempt (see DEEPER STUDY # 1—Mk.15:1-15). On several occasions, Jewish leaders threatened to exercise their right to report Pilate to the emperor. This, of course, disturbed Pilate to no end and caused him to become even more bitter and contemptuous toward the Jews.

2 (23:18-21) **Compromise**: Pilate tried to compromise the truth despite clear evidence. He saw the evidence: Jesus was innocent, and the religionists were only envious of Jesus, feeling He was a threat to their security. Pilate wanted to declare Jesus innocent, but he felt he had to satisfy the cries of these religious worldlings as well. Therefore, he conceived a compromise. It was a long time custom for Rome to release a popular prisoner to the Jews at the Passover Feast in order to humor and secure more cooperation from the population. Within the prison was a notorious criminal, Barabbas. Pilate had him brought before the people along with Jesus and shouted out that the people could choose which one was to be released.

Pilate felt sure that by pitting Barabbas against Jesus, the people would choose Jesus, the One who had ministered and helped so many of them. How wrong the man of compromise was. (The world will always cry out against Jesus to get rid of Him.)

The point to note is the moral weakness of Pilate. He knew Jesus was innocent. He knew the Jews sought to kill Jesus because they envied Him. Jesus should have been released immediately, but Pilate attempted a compromise instead of standing up for the truth.

Thought 1. Note a crucial point: when the truth is known, it should be proclaimed, not compromised. Compromise results in three tragedies.
1) Compromise weakens character and testimony.
2) Compromise means that the truth is not being done or lived. A person is agreeing to do something less than what he should be doing.
3) Compromise weakens principle, position, and life.

Thought 2. God accepts no compromise concerning His Son, Jesus Christ. A man either stands for Christ or against Christ. There is no neutral ground. Christ is innocent and sinless; He is the Ideal Man, the Son of God in whom all men are to place their trust.

> **"He who is not with me is against me, and he who does not gather with me, scatters. (Luke 11:23)**

> **That all may honor the Son just as they honor the Father. He who does not honor the Son does not honor the Father, who**

sent him. **"I tell you the truth, whoever hears my word and believes him who sent me has eternal life and will not be condemned; he has crossed over from death to life. (John 5:23-24)**

> **And this is the testimony: God has given us eternal life, and this life is in his Son. He who has the Son has life; he who does not have the Son of God does not have life. (1 John 5:11-12)**

> **Submit yourselves, then, to God. Resist the devil, and he will flee from you. Come near to God and he will come near to you. Wash your hands, you sinners, and purify your hearts, you double-minded. Grieve, mourn and wail. Change your laughter to mourning and your joy to gloom. Humble yourselves before the Lord, and he will lift you up. (James 4:7-10)**

3 (23:22-25) **Worldliness—Compromise**: Pilate gave in to worldly pressure. The scene was dramatic, but tragic. The scene can be simply stated. Pilate...
* knew Jesus was innocent (v.22).
* faced loud voices against Jesus (v.23).
* compromised and gave in to the worldly cries (v.24).
* allowed injustice and wrong and sin to be done (v.25).

The point is this: Pilate, the compromising man, was *morally weak*.
* He was not strong enough to do what he knew was right.
* He lacked the moral strength to stand up for Jesus.
* He was too weak to declare the truth.

Thought 1. The pressure of the world to do evil is great. Indecision and compromise are not the way to face the world: decisive dedication to Christ and separation from the world alone can conquer the world.

> **Therefore, I urge you, brothers, in view of God's mercy, to offer your bodies as living sacrifices, holy and pleasing to God—this is your spiritual act of worship. Do not conform any longer to the pattern of this world, but be transformed by the renewing of your mind. Then you will be able to test and approve what God's will is—his good, pleasing and perfect will. (Rom 12:1-2)**

> **"Therefore come out from them and be separate, says the Lord. Touch no unclean thing, and I will receive you." "I will be a Father to you, and you will be my sons and daughters, says the Lord Almighty." (2 Cor 6:17-18)**

> **Do not love the world or anything in the world. If anyone loves the world, the love of the Father is not in him. For everything in the world—the cravings of sinful man, the lust of his eyes and the boasting of what he has and does—comes not from the Father but from the world. (1 John 2:15-16)**

Thought 2. Most men prefer the company of evil, sinful men to that of the Prince of Life. Note: even worldly religionists choose the world over the Prince of Life.

Thought 3. Note a crucial point. It is when we are indecisive or willing to compromise that the pressure to do evil gets to us. Hesitating and being indecisive will cause us to give in to the pressure of sin.

By faith Moses, when he had grown up, refused to be known as the son of Pharaoh's daughter. He chose to be mistreated along with the people of God rather than to enjoy the pleasures of sin for a short time. (Heb 11:24-25)

Therefore, dear friends, since you already know this, be on your guard so that you may not be carried away by the error of lawless men and fall from your secure position. (2 Pet 3:17)

	G. Jesus' Crucifixion &	and mocked him. They offered	1) Offering Him vinegar
	Its Events,[DS1] **23:26-49**	him wine vinegar	wine[DS2]
	(Mt.27:26-56; Mk.15:	37 And said, "If you are the	2) His claim to be King
	16-41; Jn.19:16-37)	king of the Jews, save your-	
		self."	
1. The man who bore His cross:	26 As they led him away,	38 There was a written notice	9. **The inscription on the**
A picture of conversion	they seized Simon from	above him, which read: THIS	**cross: A misunderstood**
	Cyrene, who was on his way	IS THE KING OF THE JEWS.	**charge**
	in from the country, and put	39 One of the criminals who	10. **The unrepentant thief: A**
	the cross on him and made	hung there hurled insults at	**picture of hardness even in**
	him carry it behind Jesus.	him: "Aren't you the Christ?	**death**
2. The great crowd of mourners:	27 A large number of people	Save yourself and us!"	
A picture of hearts that felt	followed him, including	40 But the other criminal re-	11. **The repentant thief: A pic-**
for Jesus	women who mourned and	buked him. "Don't you fear	**ture of true confession**
	wailed for him.	God," he said, "since you are	a. Feared God
3. The prediction of Jerusalem's	28 Jesus turned and said to	under the same sentence?	
doom: A picture of coming	them, "Daughters of Jerusa-	41 We are punished justly, for	
judgment	lem, do not weep for me;	we are getting what our deeds	
a. So terrible, people should	weep for yourselves and for	deserve. But this man has done	b. Declared Jesus' righteous-
weep over	your children.	nothing wrong."	ness
b. So terrible, people will wish	29 For the time will come	42 Then he said, "Jesus, re-	
to be childless	when you will say, 'Blessed	member me when you come	
	are the barren women, the	into your kingdom."	
	wombs that never bore and	43 Jesus answered him, "I tell	c. Asked Jesus for a place in
c. So terrible, people will wish	the breasts that never nursed!'	you the truth, today you will be	His kingdom
to be buried alive	30 Then "'they will say to	with me in paradise."	
	the mountains, "Fall on us!"	44 It was now about the sixth	12. **The awesome darkness: A**
d. So terrible because judgment	and to the hills, "Cover us!"'	hour, and darkness came over	**symbol of separation &**
is inevitable	31 For if men do these things	the whole land until the ninth	**loneliness**
	when the tree is green, what	hour,	
	will happen when it is dry?"	45 For the sun stopped shin-	13. **The torn veil of the temple:**
4. The identification with crimi-	32 Two other men, both	ing. And the curtain of the	**A symbol of open access**
nals: Being numbered with	criminals, were also led out	temple was torn in two.	**into God's presence**
sinners	with him to be executed.	46 Jesus called out with a loud	14. **The great cry of trust: A**
5. The crucifixion: The summit	33 When they came to the	voice, "Father, into your hands	**picture of glorious triumph**
of sin & love	place called the Skull, there	I commit my spirit." When he	
a. At Mount Calvary	they crucified him, along	had said this, he breathed his	
b. Crucified between two	with the criminals—one on	last.	
criminals	his right, the other on his	47 The centurion, seeing what	15. **The centurion's declara-**
	left.	had happened, praised God and	**tion: Jesus' righteous-**
6. The prayer for His enemies:	34 Jesus said, "Father, for-	said, "Surely this was a right-	**ness—a confession to be**
Forgiveness	give them, for they do not	eous man."	**made by many**
7. The gambling for His clothes:	know what they are doing."	48 When all the people who	16. **The people's grief: A pic-**
Being stripped by greed	And they divided up his	had gathered to witness this	**ture of stricken conscience**
	clothes by casting lots.	sight saw what took place, they	
	35 The people stood watch-	beat their breasts and went	
8. The mocking: Misunder-	ing, and the rulers even	away.	
standing His salvation	sneered at him. They said,	49 But all those who knew	17. **The followers of Jesus: A**
a. Misunderstood by the people	"He saved others; let him save	him, including the women who	**proof that Jesus lived &**
& religionists	himself if he is the Christ of	had followed him from Galilee,	**served well**
1) His claim to save	God, the Chosen One."	stood at a distance, watching	
2) His claim to be Messiah	36 The soldiers also came up	these things.	
b. Misunderstood by the soldiers			

DIVISION XI

THE SON OF MAN'S SUFFERINGS: HIS AGONY, TRIALS, AND CRUCIFIXION, 22:39-23:56

G. Jesus' Crucifixion and Its Events, 23:26-49

(23:26-49) **Introduction**: the crucifixion of Jesus Christ is both the most shocking event and the most wonderful event of human history. It is the most shocking event in that it is the creature murdering the Creator. It is the most wonderful event in that it is the Creator saving the creature. (Glance at the outline above for the *seventeen events* of the crucifixion as covered by Luke.)

DEEPER STUDY # 1

(23:26-49) **Crucifixion, The**: see outline, note, and DEEPER STUDY # 1—Mt.27:26-44 for more discussion.

1 (23:26) **Conversion—Simon of Cyrene**: the man who bore His cross, a picture of conversion. Note several things.

1. God's plan or providence. Nothing happens by chance, not to the Christian believer. God oversees the life of His people. Thus, Simon's being pressed into carrying the cross for Jesus was in the plan of God.

2. Simon was apparently a pilgrim coming to celebrate the Passover. He was standing along the roadway watching the armed procession make its way through the streets. Apparently there was some expression of concern and sympathy for Jesus, something within his heart that was touched and that reached out to Jesus. God knew this, and directed the soldiers to enlist his help in carrying the Lord's cross.

3. Simon was "the father of Alexander and Rufus" (Mk.15:21). The comment by Mark is interesting. Evidently they were known believers (see Acts 13:1; Ro.16:13). The indication is that Simon or at least his two sons were eventually converted.

Thought 1. The man who takes up the cross of Christ will be converted.

> Then he said to them all: "If anyone would come after me, he must deny himself and take up his cross daily and follow me. (Luke 9:23)

2 (23:27) **Godly Sorrow—Sympathy**: there was the great crowd of mourners—a picture of hearts that felt for Jesus. A great crowd of people followed and felt for Jesus, especially women. The word "mourned" (ekoptonto) means to cut, strike, smite, beat. They were cut to the core of their hearts, actually feeling pain for Jesus. The word "wailed" (ethrenoun) means to cry out loud, to mourn, groan. They were crying out, unable to hold back the pain cutting their hearts. Some of the people, of course, had been followers of Jesus for a long time and were feeling the depth of their Lord's sufferings; whereas other onlookers, as in any crowd witnessing severe suffering, felt only a natural tenderness and lament over one suffering so much.

Thought 1. A natural response to the Lord's sufferings is not enough. A person must *understand* why Christ suffered and must feel a *godly sorrow* over Christ's having to bear the sins of the world (see DEEPER STUDY # 1—2 Cor.7:10).

> Godly sorrow brings repentance that leads to salvation and leaves no regret, but worldly sorrow brings death. (2 Cor 7:10)
> Remember those in prison as if you were their fellow prisoners, and those who are mistreated as if you yourselves were suffering. (Heb 13:3)

3 (23:28-31) **Jerusalem, Prophecy of**: there was the prediction of Jerusalem's doom—a picture of coming judgment. The significant point to note is what was upon Jesus' mind: judgment. The people had rejected God's Messiah and salvation, choosing to go the way of the world, and the way of the world was doom and destruction. The destruction coming would be so terrible, people...
* would weep for themselves.
* would wish to be childless.
* would wish to be buried alive.

Verse 31 is a proverbial saying: if the world (Rome) treats a green tree like this (Him, a tree with its full provi-sion of sap), how will it treat a dry tree like Israel, a tree with little if any provision of sap, a tree of no use, with no life left, ready to be cut down and destroyed?

Thought 1. Jerusalem rejected the invitation of God time and again. However, God was patient and demonstrated His patience for generations, but the rejection and killing of His Son were too great to leave unpunished. As soon as Christianity could get a solid foothold in the world, Jerusalem was to be judged and doomed. (See outline and notes—Lk.20:13-18.)

God is patient with every man. But continued rejection of His Son brings judgment and eternal doom.

> "For God so loved the world that he gave his one and only Son, that whoever believes in him shall not perish but have eternal life. For God did not send his Son into the world to condemn the world, but to save the world through him. Whoever believes in him is not condemned, but whoever does not believe stands condemned already because he has not believed in the name of God's one and only Son. (John 3:16-18)
> Just as man is destined to die once, and after that to face judgment, (Heb 9:27)

4 (23:32) **Jesus Christ, Identified with Sinners**: there was the identification with criminals—a picture of being numbered with sinners. Why was Jesus crucified with criminals? Scripture does not say, but perhaps this was a day set aside for execution, or perhaps the Jewish leaders pressed Pilate to execute Jesus with other criminals. By this, they hoped to add weight to their position that He was no more than a mere man, an imposter who deserved to die just as other criminals. Whatever the reason, the fact that the Son of God was executed right along with other criminals adds to the shame and reproach He bore. This event had been prophesied just as many others had (Is.53:12).

Thought 1. Christ was counted as a sinner that He might bear the sin of many.

> Therefore I will give him a portion among the great, and he will divide the spoils with the strong, because he poured out his life unto death, and was numbered with the transgressors. For he bore the sin of many, and made intercession for the transgressors. (Isa 53:12)

5 (23:33) **Crucifixion, The**: the crucifixion was the summit of sin and love. The crucifixion itself was the most horrible of deaths. There was the pain of the spikes forced through the flesh of Jesus' hands and feet or ankles. There was the weight of His body jolting and pulling against the spikes as the cross was lifted and rocked into place. There was the scorching sun and the unquenchable thirst gnawing away at His dry mouth and throat. There was the blood oozing from His scourged back, His thorn crowned brow, His stick beaten head. In addition, just imagine the aggravation of flies, gnats, and other insects. And for Jesus, there was the piercing pain of the spear thrust into His side. On and on the sufferings could be described. There has never been a more cruel form of execution than crucifixion upon a cross.

The crucifixion took place on a hill called *"the Skull"* (in Latin, calvaria). We get the name Calvary from the Latin word. (See note, pt.11—Mt.27:26-38.)

Thought 1. In the simplest of terms, Christ was crucified for our sins in order to bring us to God.

> **He himself bore our sins in his body on the tree, so that we might die to sins and live for righteousness; by his wounds you have been healed. (1 Pet 2:24)**
> **For Christ died for sins once for all, the righteous for the unrighteous, to bring you to God. He was put to death in the body but made alive by the Spirit, (1 Pet 3:18)**

Note that two criminals were crucified with Him. He was dying because of them and because of all other men. Why? Because all men are criminals against God, rebelling against Him and breaking His commandments.

> **For all have sinned and fall short of the glory of God, (Rom 3:23)**
> **Here is a trustworthy saying that deserves full acceptance: Christ Jesus came into the world to save sinners—of whom I am the worst. (1 Tim 1:15)**
> **For Christ died for sins once for all, the righteous for the unrighteous, to bring you to God. He was put to death in the body but made alive by the Spirit, (1 Pet 3:18)**

6 (23:34) **Forgiveness—Salvation**: there was the prayer for His enemies—a picture of love and forgiveness to the end. The picture is of Jesus the Mediator. He had come for this very purpose, to stand as the Mediator between God and sinful man. Therefore upon the cross, He prayed for those who stood below crucifying Him. Note several things.
1. It had been predicted that Christ would pray for transgressors (Is.53:12).
2. He prayed for God to forgive those who were crucifying Him. The very purpose for His coming was to make provision for forgiveness of sins. Because of His death, God would be able to forgive the sins of men, even those who were now crucifying Him.
3. The men crucifying Him did not know what they were doing. They did not know who He was.

> **None of the rulers of this age understood it, for if they had, they would not have crucified the Lord of glory. (1 Cor 2:8)**

Thought 1. The most wonderful truth in all the world is this: God will hold no sin against any man if that man will personally trust His Son. If God forgives the men who killed His only Son, God will forgive any man for any sin—if that man will just ask.

> **The God of our fathers raised Jesus from the dead—whom you had killed by hanging him on a tree. God exalted him to his own right hand as Prince and Savior that he might give repentance and forgiveness of sins to Israel. (Acts 5:30-31)**
> **Repent of this wickedness and pray to the Lord. Perhaps he will forgive you for**

having such a thought in your heart. (Acts 8:22)

> **"Therefore, my brothers, I want you to know that through Jesus the forgiveness of sins is proclaimed to you. Through him everyone who believes is justified from everything you could not be justified from by the law of Moses. (Acts 13:38-39)**
> **In whom we have redemption, the forgiveness of sins. (Col 1:14; see Col. 2:13)**

7 (23:34) **Mortality—Immortality**: there was the gambling for His clothes—a picture of being stripped by the selfishness, greed, and sin of men. Note two points.
1. The custom seems to have been for the executing soldiers to claim whatever they wished of the clothes of crucified criminals. The soldiers stripped Jesus, dividing His clothes among themselves. However, His coat was valuable: it was seamless, one piece of cloth, woven from top to bottom just as the High Priest's coat or cloak was. The soldiers, therefore, decided to gamble by casting lots for it (Jn.19:23-24). This event was foretold in Ps.22:18.
2. Jesus was stripped by the soldiers, stripped of His mortal clothes. There is symbolism in this act: He allowed all His mortality to be stripped so that He might abolish death and bring life and immortality to light.

> **But it [God's grace] has now been revealed through the appearing of our Savior, Christ Jesus, who has destroyed death and has brought life and immortality to light through the gospel. (2 Tim 1:10)**

8 (23:35-37) **Salvation**: there was the mockery, the misunderstanding of His salvation. Note those who mocked and taunted Him.
1. The people and religionists mocked His claim to be the Savior and Messiah. They totally misunderstood God's Messiahship. Both the people and the religionists should have been above this kind of behavior. In addition, they had every opportunity to believe, for He had not hid Himself or His message of salvation. But being part of a sinful crowd and their own unbelief, they led each other to do shameful things.

> **...Christ [Messiah] Jesus, who gave himself as a ransom for all men—the testimony given in its proper time. (1 Tim 2:5-6)**
> **Here is a trustworthy saying that deserves full acceptance: Christ Jesus came into the world to save sinners—of whom I am the worst. (1 Tim 1:15)**

Thought 1. Leaders, civil and religious, are still men. It is not the position or profession that makes a man, but the heart. A heart of unbelief and enmity, a heart willing to become a participant with the sinful crowd, will stoop to do shameful things, no matter the position or profession.

> **Look, your house is left to you desolate. (Mat 23:38)**

2. The soldiers mocked and taunted Him. In particular they mocked His claim to be King, but they did not understand His claim (Jn.18:36. See Jn.18:33-37; Mt.27:11.)

DEEPER STUDY # 2

(23:36) **Wine**: Jesus was offered drugged wine at the beginning of the crucifixion, but He refused it (Mt.27:34; Mk.15:23). He was also offered "wine" just before His death (Jn.19:29), and here the soldiers use "wine" in some form of mockery with Him.

9 (23:38) **Jesus Christ, King**: there was the inscription on the cross—a misunderstood charge. The sign placed above His head, "The King of the Jews," was intended to mock the Jewish authorities and to reproach His claim. However, God overruled and used the sign to proclaim the truth to the whole world (Lk.23:38). The very charges against Jesus proclaimed His deity and honor.

> **And being found in appearance as a man, he humbled himself and became obedient to death— even death on a cross! Therefore God exalted him to the highest place and gave him the name that is above every name, that at the name of Jesus every knee should bow, in heaven and on earth and under the earth, and every tongue confess that Jesus Christ is Lord, to the glory of God the Father. (Phil 2:8-11)**

> **To keep this command without spot or blame until the appearing of our Lord Jesus Christ, which God will bring about in his own time—God, the blessed and only Ruler, the King of kings and Lord of lords, who alone is immortal and who lives in unapproachable light, whom no one has seen or can see. To him be honor and might forever. Amen. (1 Tim 6:14-16)**

10 (23:39) **Unbelief**: there was the unrepentant thief—a picture of hardness even in death. The thieves heard the crowd mock Jesus about being the Messiah, the Savior of the world. Hanging there as criminals, guilty before God and men, they should have been searching to see if there were any chance that Jesus could have been who He claimed. They needed to be saved and forgiven. One criminal showed enormous hardness of heart. He mocked the very thought that Jesus was the Christ.

> **"For God so loved the world that he gave his one and only Son, that whoever believes in him shall not perish but have eternal life. For God did not send his Son into the world to condemn the world, but to save the world through him. Whoever believes in him is not condemned, but whoever does not believe stands condemned already because he has not believed in the name of God's one and only Son. (John 3:16-18)**

11 (23:40-43) **Salvation—Repentance**: there was the repentant thief—a picture of true repentance. The second thief demonstrated the steps to salvation and true repentance.

⇒ He feared God (v.40).
⇒ He declared that Jesus was righteous (v.41).
⇒ He asked for Jesus to remember him (v.42).

Note that Jesus promised him eternal life; the repentant man was to be with Christ in paradise *that very day*. (See DEEPER STUDY # 3, *Paradise*—Lk.16:23.)

> **"Father, I want those you have given me to be with me where I am, and to see my glory, the glory you have given me because you loved me before the creation of the world. (John 17:24)**

> **We are confident, I say, and would prefer to be away from the body and at home with the Lord. (2 Cor 5:8)**

> **I am torn between the two: I desire to depart and be with Christ, which is better by far; (Phil 1:23)**

> **Whoever serves me must follow me; and where I am, my servant also will be. My Father will honor the one who serves me. (John 12:26)**

12 (23:44) **Judgment—Man, State of**: there was the awesome darkness—a symbol of separation and loneliness. The darkness told man something (see note—Mt.27:45 for detailed discussion).

1. Man was separated from the light.

> **This is the verdict: Light has come into the world, but men loved darkness instead of light because their deeds were evil. Everyone who does evil hates the light, and will not come into the light for fear that his deeds will be exposed. (John 3:19-20)**

2. Man stood all alone. He could not see in the dark, not well. He was, so to speak, standing in the world all alone, responsible for his own behavior; and he must face God someday all alone to give an account for his behavior.

> **Just as man is destined to die once, and after that to face judgment, (Heb 9:27)**

13 (23:45) **Access—Jesus Christ, Blood**: there was the torn veil of the temple—a symbol of open access into the very presence of God. Note four facts.

1. The veil or curtain which was torn was the inner veil (katapetasma), the curtain which separated the Holy of Holies from the Holy Place. There was another veil or curtain, an outer curtain (kalumma), which separated the Holy Place from the outer court of the temple.

The Holy of Holies was the most sacred part of the temple. It was the place where the very presence of God was symbolized as dwelling in a very, very special way. It was closed *forever* to everyone except the High Priest. Even he could enter the Holy of Holies only once a year, on the Day of Atonement (Ex.26:33).

2. At the very hour that Jesus died, the High Priest would be rolling back the outer curtain in order to expose the Holy Place to the people who had gathered to worship in the surrounding court. As he rolled back the outer curtain exposing the Holy Place for worship, both he and the worshippers would stand in amazement. Why? Because they would see the inner veil or curtain rent from the top to the bottom. There they would stand, experiencing and witnessing the Holy of Holies, the very special place where the presence of God Himself was supposed to dwell— a sight that the people had never seen before.

3. The veil or curtain was torn from top to bottom. This symbolized that it was torn by an act of God Himself. It symbolized God's giving direct access into His presence (Heb.6:19; 9:3-12, 24; 10:19-23). Now, through the body of Christ, any man can enter the presence of God anytime, anyplace.

> **And by that will, we have been made holy through the sacrifice of the body of Jesus Christ once for all. (Heb 10:10)**

4. The torn veil or curtain symbolized that all men could now draw near God by the blood of Christ.

> **But now in Christ Jesus you who once were far away have been brought near through the blood of Christ. For he himself is our peace, who has made the two one and has destroyed the barrier, the dividing wall of hostility, (Eph 2:13-14)**

14 (23:46) **Jesus Christ, Work—Purpose**: there was the great cry of trust—a picture of glorious triumph. What Jesus cried out was one word in the Greek, *Tetelestai*, "It is finished" (Jn.19:30). It was a cry of purpose, a shout of triumph. He was dying for a specific purpose and that purpose was now fulfilled (see note—Mt.27:50 for detailed discussion).

> **I am the gate; whoever enters through me will be saved. He will come in and go out, and find pasture. "I am the good shepherd. The good shepherd lays down his life for the sheep. just as the Father knows me and I know the Father—and I lay down my life for the sheep. The reason my Father loves me is that I lay down my life—only to take it up again. No one takes it from me, but I lay it down of my own accord. I have authority to lay it down and authority to take it up again. This command I received from my Father." (John 10:9, 11, 15, 17-18)**

15 (23:47) **Confession**: there was the centurion's declaration—Jesus' righteousness, a picture of the confession to be made by many.

1. The centurion was bound to be a thoughtful and honest man. He was in charge of the crucifixion, which means he was responsible for overseeing all that took place. As the events unfolded upon the cross, he was stricken more and more with the claim of Jesus and the way in which the events were happening. When Jesus shouted out that His purpose was finished, that His death was the climax of His purpose upon earth, the centurion was convinced. The very fact that Jesus' death was purposeful was the clincher. God quickened to the soldier's heart the glorious truth: "Surely this was a righteous man."

2. The centurion was a Gentile. He symbolized all who were to confess Christ in coming generations.

> **That if you confess with your mouth, "Jesus is Lord," and believe in your heart that God raised him from the dead, you will be saved. For it is with your heart that you believe and are justified, and it is with your mouth that you confess and are saved. (Rom 10:9-10)**

16 (23:48) **Preparation—Conscience**: there was the people's grief—a picture of stricken consciences. The people had come for entertainment, but they went away with saddened, grieving hearts. God, being the Sovereign Lord of the universe, saw to it that they were stricken in conscience. They were being prepared for the preaching to come after Pentecost.

> **How much more, then, will the blood of Christ, who through the eternal Spirit offered himself unblemished to God, cleanse our consciences from acts that lead to death, so that we may serve the living God! (Heb 9:14)**

17 (23:49) **Self-Denial**: there were the followers of Jesus—a proof that Jesus lived and served well. Note that the women were at the cross despite the danger. They were off, some distance away, but they were there nevertheless. They still loved and cared, no matter what. They symbolized that Jesus' life was not in vain.

> **For whoever wants to save his life will lose it, but whoever loses his life for me and for the gospel will save it. (Mark 8:35)**

| 1. A secret believer stirred to step forward for Jesus
a. A counselor
b. A good & upright man
c. A man who had feared to stand up for Jesus sometime before (Jn.19:38)
d. A man who looked for the Messiah—for God's kingdom
e. A man who was changed by the death of Jesus | H. Jesus' Burial: A Secret Disciple Stirred to Step Forth, 23:50-56 (Mt.27:57-61; Mk.15:42-47; Jn.19:38-42)

50 Now there was a man named Joseph, a member of the Council, a good and upright man,
51 Who had not consented to their decision and action. He came from the Judean town of Arimathea and he was waiting for the kingdom of God.
52 Going to Pilate, he asked for Jesus' body. | 53 Then he took it down, wrapped it in linen cloth and placed it in a tomb cut in the rock, one in which no one had yet been laid.
54 It was Preparation Day, and the Sabbath was about to begin.
55 The women who had come with Jesus from Galilee followed Joseph and saw the tomb and how his body was laid in it.
56 Then they went home and prepared spices and perfumes. But they rested on the Sabbath in obedience to the commandment. | f. A man who cared deeply for Jesus
  1) He took care of Jesus' body

  2) He acted quickly

2. The women stirred to loyalty & affection
a. Showed a fearless loyalty
b. Showed deep affection

c. Showed an ignorance of the resurrection |

DIVISION XI

THE SON OF MAN'S SUFFERINGS: HIS AGONY, TRIALS, AND CRUCIFIXION, 22:39–23:56

H. Jesus' Burial: A Secret Disciple Stirred to Step Forth, 23:50-56

(23:50-56) **Introduction**: a secret believer is a tragedy. In a sense he is the tragedy of tragedies, for he fails to confess Jesus publicly. He ignores the fact of what Jesus said: all persons are lost (Mt.10:32-33). Joseph of Arimathea was such a man: a secret believer until the death of Jesus. But the death of Jesus changed him.

1. A secret believer stirred to step forward for Jesus (vv.50-54).
2. The women stirred to loyalty and affection (vv.55-56).

1 (23:50-54) **Discipleship, Secret—Profession—Believer—Jesus Christ, Death**: the secret believer, Joseph of Arimathea, was stirred to step forward for Jesus. A revealing description is given about Joseph.

1. He was a member of the council, a senator, a member of the Sanhedrin, the ruling body of Israel. Apparently he was

- highly educated
- highly esteemed
- well liked
- very responsible
- capable of leadership

2. He was a "good and upright" man. He was a man...

- of good quality
- of high morals
- of feelings
- of compassion
- of justice
- of decision
- of truth
- of law

3. He was a man looking for the Messiah and the Kingdom of God (see notes—Lk.2:25-27; Deeper Study # 3—Mt.19:23-24).
4. He was, however, a man who feared to stand up for Jesus. John says he was "a disciple of Jesus, but secretly because he feared the Jews" (Jn.19:38). Joseph probably had met Jesus and arranged private meetings with Him when the Lord had visited Jerusalem, but he feared making a public profession. His position and prestige were at stake. His peers, the other rulers, opposed Jesus. He believed in Jesus, but out of fear he kept his discipleship a secret. Note: when the vote was taken to put Jesus to death, Joseph did abstain from voting, but he did not stand

up for Jesus. He did not participate; he simply remained silent.

Thought 1. How many persons are like Joseph? They are believers and good and upright people; however they fear what their friends and fellow workers will say. They fear the loss of position, prestige, promotion, acceptance, popularity, friends, job, income, livelihood.

> **If anyone is ashamed of me and my words, the Son of Man will be ashamed of him when he comes in his glory and in the glory of the Father and of the holy angels. (Luke 9:26)**
> **"I tell you, my friends, do not be afraid of those who kill the body and after that can do no more. But I will show you whom you should fear: Fear him who, after the killing of the body, has power to throw you into hell. Yes, I tell you, fear him. (Luke 12:4-5)**
> **For God did not give us a spirit of timidity, but a spirit of power, of love and of self-discipline. (2 Tim 1:7)**
> **Fear of man will prove to be a snare, but whoever trusts in the LORD is kept safe. (Prov 29:25)**
> **"I, even I, am he who comforts you. Who are you that you fear mortal men, the sons of men, who are but grass, (Isa 51:12)**

5. He was a man changed by the death of Jesus. This is seen in two facts.
   a. Joseph actually went to Pilate and begged for the body of Jesus. This was a tremendous act of courage. The Romans either dumped the bodies of crucified criminals in the trash heaps or left the bodies hanging upon the cross for the vultures and animals to consume. The latter served as an example of criminal punishment to the public. Joseph also braved the threat of Pilate's reaction. Pilate was fed up with the *Jesus matter*. Jesus had

proven to be very bothersome to him. He could have reacted severely against Joseph.

    b. Joseph risked the disfavor and discipline of the Sanhedrin. They were the ruling body who had instigated and condemned Jesus, and Joseph was a member of the council. There was no question—he would face some harsh reaction from some of his fellow Sanhedrin members and from some of his closest friends.

The thing that turned Joseph from being a secret disciple to a bold disciple seems to be the cross, the phenomenal events surrounding the cross (the behavior and words of Jesus, the darkness, the earthquake, the torn veil or curtain and other events). When Joseph witnessed all this, his mind connected the claims of Jesus with the Old Testament prophecies of the Messiah. Joseph saw the prophecies fulfilled in Jesus. He stepped forward braving all risks and took his stand for Jesus. A remarkable courage! A courage stirred by the death of Jesus.

Thought 1. Every secret believer needs to study the cross of Christ. Really seeing the cross will turn any secret believer into a bold witness for Christ.

Thought 2. Joseph courageously asked to take care of the physical body of Christ. Today, the body of Christ is the church. We are to boldly step forward and take care of the church. There are special times of need within the church when special courage is needed to step forward and show care. In those times a fresh look at the cross will be helpful and can be used by God to stir us.

    So I made up my mind that I would not make another painful visit to you. (2 Cor 2:1)

    Because we know that the one who raised the Lord Jesus from the dead will also raise us with Jesus and present us with you in his presence. All this is for your benefit, so that the grace that is reaching more and more people may cause thanksgiving to overflow to the glory of God. (2 Cor 4:14-15)

    And he died for all, that those who live should no longer live for themselves but for him who died for them and was raised again. (2 Cor 5:15)

6. He was a man who cared deeply for Jesus. The words and acts of these two verses express care and tenderness, love and affection, as well as courage and boldness. Joseph...
* took the Lord's body down from the cross.
* wrapped the body in linen.
* laid the body in a tomb, a tomb in which no man had ever been laid.
* acted quickly, before the Sabbath began. Jesus died at 3 p.m. Friday afternoon which was the day of preparation for the Sabbath (see Mk.15:33-34, 37). Work was forbidden on the Sabbath, so if anything was to be done with Jesus' body, it had to be done immediately. Only three hours remained for work. (See note—Mk.15:42 for more discussion.)

This act alone would leave no doubt about the effect of the cross upon Joseph. The cross changed his life. He was no longer a secret believer; he now demonstrated a public stand for Jesus.

Thought 1. Position, power, wealth, fame—none of these can make us bold for Christ. Only true affection for Christ will make us bold, and only as we see the cross of Christ will affection for Christ be aroused.

Thought 2. Christ identified with men perfectly.
  ⇒ He lived as a man—but perfectly.
  ⇒ He died as a man—but perfectly (as the Ideal Man).
  ⇒ He was buried as a man—but perfectly.

    He was assigned a grave with the wicked, and with the rich in his death, though he had done no violence, nor was any deceit in his mouth. (Isa 53:9)

    For this reason he had to be made like his brothers in every way, in order that he might become a merciful and faithful high priest in service to God, and that he might make atonement for the sins of the people. (Heb 2:17)

Thought 3. God's own Son possessed nothing when He was on earth; therefore when He died, He had to be buried in a borrowed tomb. Note two things.
  ⇒ Christ is the Savior of the poorest. He was born in a stable. He had no place of His own to lay His head (Mt.8:20; Lk.9:58). His tomb was a borrowed tomb.
  ⇒ Yet the rich can serve Him just as Joseph of Arimathea did.

    Jesus replied, "Foxes have holes and birds of the air have nests, but the Son of Man has no place to lay his head." (Luke 9:58)

    Sell your possessions and give to the poor. Provide purses for yourselves that will not wear out, a treasure in heaven that will not be exhausted, where no thief comes near and no moth destroys. (Luke 12:33)

    In everything I did, I showed you that by this kind of hard work we must help the weak, remembering the words the Lord Jesus himself said: 'It is more blessed to give than to receive.'" (Acts 20:35)

    For you know the grace of our Lord Jesus Christ, that though he was rich, yet for your sakes he became poor, so that you through his poverty might become rich. (2 Cor 8:9)

    This is how we know what love is: Jesus Christ laid down his life for us. And we ought to lay down our lives for our brothers. (1 John 3:16)

2 (23:55-56) **Jesus Christ, Love for—Eternal Life**: the women believers were stirred to loyalty and affection. Note three facts.

1. The women demonstrated a fearless loyalty despite all danger. At the cross the men forsook Jesus, but not the women (Mt.26:56, 69-75; see Mt.27:55-56, 61; Mk.15:41).

2. The women demonstrated a deep affection for Jesus. They took their own money to buy spices and perfumes to embalm Jesus. This they did because they loved Him (Lk.23:56; see Mt.27:61; Mk.16:1).

3. The women did not yet understand the resurrection of Jesus. They were preparing His body to lie and eventually to decay in the tomb. The true meaning of *living forever—the human body being remade, recreated, and becoming incorruptible—*had not yet been grasped by them (Jn.5:24-29; see 1 Cor.15:42f. See 1 Cor.15:1-58.)

Thought 1. The testimony of these women should stir men to stand up for Christ. Too often it is the women who take the lead in standing forth for Christ. This should not be the case. Men...
- should be loyal to Christ, no matter how grave the danger.
- should love Christ to such an extent that they give all they *are and have* to Christ.
- should seek to understand and grasp the resurrection of Christ in all its fullness.

So do not be ashamed to testify about our Lord, or ashamed of me his prisoner. But join with me in suffering for the gospel, by the power of God, (2 Tim 1:8)

I am not ashamed of the gospel, because it is the power of God for the salvation of everyone who believes: first for the Jew, then for the Gentile. (Rom 1:16)

	CHAPTER 24	dead?	
		6 He is not here; he has	c. Their proclamation
	XII. THE SON OF MAN'S	risen! Remember how he told	d. Their reminder of Jesus'
	GLORY: HIS	you, while he was still with	prophecy
	RESURRECTION &	you in Galilee:	
	ASCENSION, 24:1-53	7 'The Son of Man must be	
		delivered into the hands of	
	A. Jesus' Empty Tomb: Its	sinful men, be crucified and	
	Discovery, 24:1-12	on the third day be raised	
	(see Mt.28:1-15; Mk.16:	again.'"	
	1-11; Jn.20:1-18)	8 Then they remembered his	
		words.	
1. The first day of the week	On the first day of the week,	9 When they came back from	**6. The immediate unbelief of the**
2. The first witness of the resur-	very early in the morning, the	the tomb, they told all these	**apostles**
rection	women took the spices they	things to the Eleven and to all	
	had prepared and went to the	the others.	
	tomb.	10 It was Mary Magdalene,	a. The message of the resurrec-
3. The great stone rolled away	2 They found the stone rolled	Joanna, Mary the mother of	tion was carried by women—
	away from the tomb,	James, and the others with	initially
4. The body missing from the	3 But when they entered,	them who told this to the	
tomb	they did not find the body of	apostles.	
	the Lord Jesus.	11 But they did not believe	b. The message of the resurrec-
5. The two angels & their unbe-	4 While they were wonder-	the women, because their	tion was perceived as non-
lievable message	ing about this, suddenly two	words seemed to them like	sense & denied
a. Their dazzling clothes	men in clothes that gleamed	nonsense.	
	like lightning stood beside	12 Peter, however, got up	**7. The continued unbelief of**
	them.	and ran to the tomb. Bending	**Peter**
b. Their question	5 In their fright the women	over, he saw the strips of	a. He ran to see—hopeful
	bowed down with their faces	linen lying by themselves,	b. He saw evidence: Linen
	to the ground, but the men	and he went away, wondering	clothes folded & off to the
	said to them, "Why do you	to himself what had hap-	side
	look for the living among the	pened.	c. He wondered

DIVISION XII

THE SON OF MAN'S GLORY: HIS
RESURRECTION AND ASCENSION, 24:1-53

A. Jesus' Empty Tomb: Its Discovery, 24:1-12

(24:1-12) **Introduction**: the tomb was empty. Discovering the empty tomb was the greatest discovery in human history. However, the great tragedy is that most people either are not aware that Jesus arose or do not believe that He arose. Every man has to discover the fact for himself. The empty tomb and the risen Lord have to become a personal discovery for every man.

1. The first day of the week (v.1).
2. The first witness of the resurrection (v.1).
3. The great stone rolled away (v.2).
4. The body missing from the tomb (v.3).
5. The two angels and their unbelievable message (vv.4-8).
6. The immediate unbelief of the apostles (vv.9-11).
7. The continued unbelief of Peter (v.12).

1 (24:1) **Jesus Christ, Resurrection**: the first day of the week, Sunday, was the day upon which Jesus arose, the day after the Jewish Sabbath (Saturday). Note three facts.

1. Luke clearly spells out when Jesus arose: "On the first day of the week, very early in the morning." Jesus arose before dawn, before the sun arose on Sunday morning. This was significant to the early Christian believers, so significant that they broke away from the common day for worship during the week, the Sabbath or Saturday. They began to worship on Sunday, the day of the resurrection of their Lord (see Acts 20:7; 1 Cor.16:2).

2. Jesus arose on the first day of the week, on Sunday morning. This means that He had been in the grave for three days just as He had said (Mt.12:40; 16:21; 17:23; 20:19; Mk.9:31; 10:34; Lk.9:22; 18:33; 24:7, 46). His resurrection from the dead was a triumph, a conquest over death. Death reigns no more—its rule has been broken (1 Cor.15:55-56; 2 Cor.1:9-10; 2 Tim.1:10; Heb.2:9, 14-15).

3. Again, Jesus arose on the first day of the week, Sunday morning. He was in the grave on the Sabbath, unable to observe the laws governing the great season of the Passover and the Sabbath. He was dead; therefore, the law and its observances had no authority over Him. This is symbolic of the *identification* believers gain in Christ. When a man believes in Jesus Christ, God identifies the man with Christ, in particular with the death of Christ. God counts the man as having died with Christ. Very simply, *in Christ's death* believers become dead to the law (see notes—Ro.7:4; Mt.5:17-18 for more discussion).

2 (24:1) **Jesus Christ, Resurrection**: the first witnesses of resurrection provide strong evidence of the resurrection.

1. They were actual witnesses of Jesus' *death and burial*. They knew He was dead, and they knew where He had been laid. They had followed along behind the procession to the tomb (Mt.15:40-41, 47; see Mt.27:55-56, 61; Lk.23:55-56). There was no question whatsoever in their mind about His being dead and buried.

2. They had purchased spices and had *come to anoint* Jesus' body. Apparently they had bought the spices Saturday evening after 6 p.m. when the Sabbath ended. Note: they arose "very early in the morning, the first day of the week [Sunday]" to go and embalm Him. Again, they knew He was dead, and they cared; so they wanted to take care of His body just as loved ones care for the bodies of their deceased.

3. They were religionists who *strictly obeyed the law*. They were strict in the observance of the Sabbath. Imagine—their loved one was dead, yet they would not break the Sabbath law even to take care of Him (see Lk.23:56). The women were obedient to the commandments of God. They were *moral and truthful* and would never think, much less consider, lying about the death and resurrection of Jesus.

3 (24:2) **Jesus Christ, Resurrection**: there was the great stone rolled away from the entrance (see DEEPER STUDY # 1, *Stone*—Mt.27:65-66). The rolled away stone perplexed the women (v.4). However, the stone had not been rolled back for the benefit of Jesus, but for the witnesses to the resurrection. When Jesus arose, He was in His resurrection body, the heavenly body of the spiritual dimension; and the spiritual dimension has no physical bounds. But the witnesses needed to enter the tomb and see the truth (see outline and notes—Jn.20:1-10).

4 (24:3) **Jesus Christ, Resurrection**: there was the body missing from the tomb. The account is simple, yet striking: "when they entered they did not find the body of the Lord Jesus." They saw, contemplated that Jesus was not there (Mk.16:6). They saw the slab upon which He had been laid, and *He was not there*.

> **Being fully persuaded that God had power to do what he had promised. (Rom 4:21)**
>
> **For no matter how many promises God has made, they are "Yes" in Christ. And so through him the "Amen" is spoken by us to the glory of God. (2 Cor 1:20)**
>
> **If we are faithless, he will remain faithful, for he cannot disown himself. (2 Tim 2:13)**
>
> **Through these he has given us his very great and precious promises, so that through them you may participate in the divine nature and escape the corruption in the world caused by evil desires. (2 Pet 1:4)**

5 (24:4-8) **Angels—Jesus Christ, Resurrection**: there were the two angels and their message. Note four significant points about the angels.

1. The angels were radiant, dazzling figures. Their clothes shone (Mt.28:3)...
   - "like lightning" (visible, quick, startling, striking, frightening, brilliant).
   - "white as snow" (pure, glistening).

Note the women feared and fell down, bowing in reverence.

2. The angels asked a pointed question: "Why do you look for the living among the dead?" There was a rebuke in the question. They were seeking to honor a dead Savior, a Savior who was as all other men are, frail and powerless

to do anything about life and eternity. Their whole being—their thoughts, feelings, and behavior—were focused upon a dead Savior.

They were living just as the world lives—"foreigners to the covenants of the promise, without hope, and without God in the world" (Eph.2:12).

3. The angels proclaimed the glorious news: "He is not here, but he has risen." Note two points.
   a. "He is not here": the women could see and did see the fact. The fact was clearly evident: Jesus was not in the tomb. He had been there, for the women had seen Him put there. They had witnessed His death and burial, but He was no longer in the tomb (see note—Lk.23:55-56).
   b. "He has risen." Startling, unbelievable words...
      - yet, heaven "declares Him to be living" (Heb.7:8).
      - yet, Scripture witnesses that He arose (Ro.1:4; Eph.1:19-20).
      - yet, He had foretold that He would arise (Lk.9:22; 13:32; 17:25; 18:31-34).

> **And who through the Spirit of holiness was declared with power to be the Son of God by his resurrection from the dead: Jesus Christ our Lord. (Rom 1:4)**
>
> **And his incomparably great power for us who believe. That power is like the working of his mighty strength, which he exerted in Christ when he raised him from the dead and seated him at his right hand in the heavenly realms, (Eph 1:19-20)**

4. The angels reminded the women that Jesus had foretold His death and resurrection (see outline and notes—Lk.18:31-34). Note the words, "Then they remembered His words." The followers of Jesus had always been confused about the prophecy of His death and resurrection. They *would not* accept his words literally, refusing to take His predictions at face value. They symbolized His statements; therefore, they never understood His death and resurrection (see note—Lk.18:34).

But note what happened now. They knew they had been wrong. Conviction struck them, and they became the very first witnesses to the resurrection.

> **Jesus looked at them and said, "With man this is impossible, but with God all things are possible." (Mat 19:26)**
>
> **For nothing is impossible with God." (Luke 1:37)**
>
> **God, who has called you into fellowship with his Son Jesus Christ our Lord, is faithful. (1 Cor 1:9)**
>
> **If we are faithless, he will remain faithful, for he cannot disown himself. (2 Tim 2:13)**
>
> **Let us hold unswervingly to the hope we profess, for he who promised is faithful. (Heb 10:23)**

6 (24:9-11) **Unbelief—Disciples**: the immediate unbelief of the disciples. The women rushed to the disciples to share the glorious news. But the news "seemed to them as like nonsense (hos leros): idle tales, ridiculous talk, wild imagination. "They did not believe the women." The

Greek word is *disbelieved* (epistoun) and is in the imperfect active tense which means they *"kept on disbelieving,"* kept on putting no trust or confidence in what the women were claiming. They were *gripped* with a skeptical, unbelieving spirit.

Thought 1. The disciples were without excuse. Christ had spent month after month drilling His death and resurrection into His disciples. (See notes—Mt.16:21-28; 17:1-13; 17:22; 17:24-27 for more discussion.)

> Later Jesus appeared to the Eleven as they were eating; he rebuked them for their lack of faith and their stubborn refusal to believe those who had seen him after he had risen. (Mark 16:14)
> Whoever believes in him is not condemned, but whoever does not believe stands condemned already because he has not believed in the name of God's one and only Son. (John 3:18)
> See to it, brothers, that none of you has a sinful, unbelieving heart that turns away from the living God. (Heb 3:12)
> Let us, therefore, make every effort to enter that rest, so that no one will fall by following their example of disobedience. (Heb 4:11)

7 (24:12) **Unbelief—Peter:** the continued unbelief of Peter. Peter's heart was still drawn to the Lord despite his enormous failure. Hearing that the body of Jesus was no longer in the tomb, he rushed to the tomb with his thoughts flying, wondering what had happened to the Lord.

Note a crucial point. Peter stooped down and saw the evidence: the linen clothes were lying off to the side by themselves. However, Peter did not grasp the significance of the evidence. John said he had rushed to the tomb with Peter and did believe, based upon the evidence of the linen clothes. He also verifies that Peter did not grasp the significance at this point (see note—Jn.20:1-10 for a discussion of this significant point). Peter just "went away," wondering within himself what had really happened.

Thought 1. It is dangerous not to understand the Lord's Word, not to take His Word at face value. Spiritualizing His words, unless the words are clearly symbolic, often leads to serious unbelief and problems.

Thought 2. A person has to be open to the evidence of the resurrection. The tomb is empty; He is risen—and the honest and seeking man will be convinced by the Spirit of God. What is needed is to do as Peter did: run to the tomb to see what really did happen.

> He said to them, "How foolish you are, and how slow of heart to believe all that the prophets have spoken! (Luke 24:25)
> He said to his disciples, "Why are you so afraid? Do you still have no faith?" (Mark 4:40)
> Whoever believes in the Son has eternal life, but whoever rejects the Son will not see life, for God's wrath remains on him." (John 3:36)
> I told you that you would die in your sins; if you do not believe that I am the one I claim to be, you will indeed die in your sins." (John 8:24)

B. Jesus' Appearance to Two Believers on the Road to Emmaus: An Immortal Journey, 24:13-35

(Mk.16:12-13)

1. **Scene 1: Two disciples taking a lonely but thoughtful walk**[DS1]
   a. They had heard about the resurrection: "That same day"
   b. They thought about & discussed the events
2. **Scene 2: Considering three critical questions**
   a. Jesus drew near, but they did not recognize Him

   b. Jesus 1st question: What are you talking about?
      1) Attitude: Gloomy

      2) Answer: The things that have happened

   c. Jesus 2nd question: What events?
      1) Jesus' death
         a) He was a great prophet

         b) He was crucified

         c) He was thought to be the Messiah
      2) Jesus' prophecy of three days

      3) Jesus' empty tomb & perplexing reports

         a) Reports of visions
         b) Reports of Jesus' being alive

   c) Reports confirmed

   d. Question 3: Did not the prophets predict the Messiah's death & resurrection?
      1) Jesus mildly rebuked them
      2) Jesus' death & resurrection were necessary

      3) Jesus explained the Scripture

3. **Scene 3: Experiencing the burning truth—Jesus is risen; He is alive**

   a. The two sought to hear more: Invited Him to stay with them
      1) He accepted the invitation

      2) He blessed the food

   b. God opened their eyes: They knew the Lord, but He disappeared from their sight

   c. They had experienced conviction: A burning within their hearts

4. **Scene 4: Proclaiming the immortal witness**
   a. The two rushed to the disciples

   b. The exciting meeting, the immortal witness: Christ is risen
      1) Had been seen by Simon
      2) Had been seen by the two from Emmaus

13 Now that same day two of them were going to a village called Emmaus, about seven miles from Jerusalem. 14 They were talking with each other about everything that had happened. 15 As they talked and discussed these things with each other, Jesus himself came up and walked along with them; 16 But they were kept from recognizing him. 17 He asked them, "What are you discussing together as you walk along?" They stood still, their faces downcast. 18 One of them, named Cleopas, asked him, "Are you only a visitor to Jerusalem and do not know the things that have happened there in these days?" 19 "What things?" he asked. "About Jesus of Nazareth," they replied. "He was a prophet, powerful in word and deed before God and all the people. 20 The chief priests and our rulers handed him over to be sentenced to death, and they crucified him; 21 But we had hoped that he was the one who was going to redeem Israel. And what is more, it is the third day since all this took place. 22 In addition, some of our women amazed us. They went to the tomb early this morning 23 But didn't find his body. They came and told us that they had seen a vision of angels, who said he was alive. 24 Then some of our companions went to the tomb and found it just as the women had said, but him they did not see." 25 He said to them, "How foolish you are, and how slow of heart to believe all that the prophets have spoken! 26 Did not the Christ have to suffer these things and then enter his glory?" 27 And beginning with Moses and all the Prophets, he explained to them what was said in all the Scriptures concerning himself. 28 As they approached the village to which they were going, Jesus acted as if he were going farther. 29 But they urged him strongly, "Stay with us, for it is nearly evening; the day is almost over." So he went in to stay with them. 30 When he was at the table with them, he took bread, gave thanks, broke it and began to give it to them. 31 Then their eyes were opened and they recognized him, and he disappeared from their sight. 32 They asked each other, "Were not our hearts burning within us while he talked with us on the road and opened the Scriptures to us?" 33 They got up and returned at once to Jerusalem. There they found the Eleven and those with them, assembled together 34 And saying, "It is true! The Lord has risen and has appeared to Simon." 35 Then the two told what had happened on the way, and how Jesus was recognized by them when he broke the bread.

DIVISION XII

THE SON OF MAN'S GLORY: HIS RESURRECTION AND ASCENSION, 24:1-53

B. Jesus' Appearance to Two Believers on the Road to Emmaus: An Immortal Journey, 24:13-35

(24:13-35) **Introduction**: this is one of the most beloved accounts of the resurrection story. It is an account of Jesus' helping two ordinary persons who had lost hope and fallen into the pit of sadness and despair. Their experience was an immortal journey.

1. Scene 1: two disciples taking a lonely but thoughtful walk (vv.13-14).
2. Scene 2: considering three critical questions (vv.15-27).
3. Scene 3: experiencing the burning truth—Jesus is risen; He is alive (vv.28-32).
4. Scene 4: proclaiming the immortal witness (vv.33-35).

1 (24:13-14) **Hopelessness—Despair—Devastation**: the first scene was that of a lonely walk by two persons—two persons who were sad, despairing, and very thoughtful.

The day is important: it was "that same day" that the women discovered the empty tomb and reported it to the disciples (the resurrection day, Easter Sunday). The news had been received with skepticism, as utter nonsense. These two, Cleopas and his companion, had either been present or else had heard the news from some other source. As they made their way to Emmaus they were sad, gripped by a spirit of despair over the Lord's crucifixion. Their hope that Jesus was the promised Messiah had been devastated, dashed against the rocks of death. But in their despair, their thoughts were rushing wildly about, entangled, wondering about the report of the women concerning the empty tomb and the angels. What did it mean?

The point to note is their emotions and thoughts, their...
- sadness and despair (over the Lord's death).
- devastated hope (He is not the Messiah).
- rushing and entangled thoughts (over the reports of an empty tomb and angels).

Thought 1. The scene is a symbol of the despair that grips so many in life. Their hopes are devastated, hopes for...
- family
- school
- meaning and purpose
- profession
- acceptance

In their sadness and despair, somewhere, they hear reports of the empty tomb and of the living Lord; but they do not know what the reports mean, not personally.

> **"I loathe my very life; therefore I will give free rein to my complaint and speak out in the bitterness of my soul. (Job 10:1)**
>
> **My life is consumed by anguish and my years by groaning; my strength fails because of my affliction, and my bones grow weak. (Psa 31:10)**
>
> **My God. My soul is downcast within me; therefore I will remember you from the land of the Jordan, the heights of Hermon—from Mount Mizar. (Psa 42:6)**
>
> **I sink in the miry depths, where there is no foothold. I have come into the deep waters; the floods engulf me. (Psa 69:2)**
>
> **But as for me, my feet had almost slipped; I had nearly lost my foothold. (Psa 73:2)**
>
> **When I tried to understand all this, it was oppressive to me (Psa 73:16)**
>
> **By the rivers of Babylon we sat and wept when we remembered Zion. (Psa 137:1)**
>
> **But Zion said, "The LORD has forsaken me, the Lord has forgotten me." (Isa 49:14)**
>
> **Do not run until your feet are bare and your throat is dry. But you said, 'It's no use! I love foreign gods, and I must go after them.' (Jer 2:25)**
>
> **Brothers, we do not want you to be ignorant about those who fall asleep [dead], or to grieve like the rest of men, who have no hope. (1 Th 4:13)**
>
> **Remember that at that time you were separate from Christ, excluded from citizenship in Israel and foreigners to the covenants of the promise, without hope and without God in the world. (Eph 2:12)**

DEEPER STUDY # 1
(24:13) **Emmaus**: the city and location are unknown. It was about seven miles out of Jerusalem, which would take somewhere around two hours to travel by foot.

2 (24:15-27) **Jesus Christ, Death—Misconception—Puzzlement—Questioning—Perplexity**: the second scene was consideration of three questions. Note the exact words as Cleopas and his companion walked along: "As they talked and discussed these things with each other, Jesus himself came up and walked along with them;" (suneporeueto, imperfect tense). The idea is that they were so absorbed in their despair and talk that Jesus *was already* walking along with them when they noticed Him. But note: they did not know Him. His resurrected body differed enough that He was not recognized as Jesus without close observation (see DEEPER STUDY # 1—Jn.21:1). In this particular instance, the Lord "kept" (restrained) their eyes from recognizing Him as well. Apparently He wanted them to more freely discuss the events with Him.

1. The first question: What are you talking about; what is it that is causing you to look so sad (skuthropoi)? The Greek word means gloomy, dejected, despondent, sullen, overcast. Jesus could see sadness and despair written all over their faces.

Cleopas was surprised that the stranger did not know. "How could anyone be in Jerusalem and not know why we are sad and despairing?" he asked. Terrible things had happened.

> **Thought 1.** These two were seeking to understand the death and empty tomb of Christ. Christ was the subject of their conversation. They were seeking the truth; therefore, Christ drew near them.
>
> **"Ask and it will be given to you; seek and you will find; knock and the door will be opened to you. For everyone who asks receives; he who seeks finds; and to him who knocks, the door will be opened. (Mat 7:7-8)**
>
> **To the Jews who had believed him, Jesus said, "If you hold to my teaching, you are really my disciples. Then you will know the truth, and the truth will set you free." (John 8:31-32)**

2. The second question: "What things? What circumstances could possibly cause such sadness and despair?" (vv.19-24). Cleopas answered, covering three subjects.
   a. Jesus' death.
   ⇒ He was a great prophet.
   ⇒ The rulers crucified him. (Note the whole world is implicated. The Jews delivered Him, and the Gentile Romans condemned and crucified Him.)
   ⇒ We had trusted (elpizomen, hoped) that He was the Messiah, the One who was to save Israel.

   b. Jesus' prophecy of three days. There is significance in the term "the third day." Cleopas was sharing how their *dead Master* had told them...
   - to watch for the third day, for some unusual event.
   - that He had spoken of "rising again on the third day," whatever that meant.

- that they thought the words meant that His triumph would take place on the third day. (See outline and notes—Lk.18:31-34 for more discussion.)

c. Jesus' empty tomb and perplexing reports from certain women, reports...
- of an empty tomb
- of a vision of angels
- of Jesus' being alive
- that had been confirmed
- that Jesus was not seen

Thought 1. World events and the terrible things that happen in life often make a person sad and despairing—such things as...

• being misunderstood	• hopelessness
• being opposed	• divisiveness
• being deserted	• loss
• being betrayed	• fear
• helplessness	• injustice
• death	

Christ is concerned. He wants to know what it is that causes so much sadness and despair. He wants us to share our problems with Him.

Thought 2. The problem with the two from Emmaus, as it is with so many today, was their *short-sightedness* and *unbelief*.

Thought 3. There is one major reason why men refuse to accept a risen Lord. A risen Lord means that a man must subject himself to the Lord and obey and serve Him.

> **"Therefore let all Israel be assured of this: God has made this Jesus, whom you crucified, both Lord and Christ." (Acts 2:36)**
>
> **God exalted him to his own right hand as Prince and Savior that he might give repentance and forgiveness of sins to Israel. We are witnesses of these things, and so is the Holy Spirit, whom God has given to those who obey him." (Acts 5:31-32)**
>
> **Therefore God exalted him to the highest place and gave him the name that is above every name, (Phil 2:9)**

Thought 4. Every man should be engrossed in the death of Christ, but he should also believe and be engrossed in the resurrection of the Lord.

> **He was delivered over to death for our sins and was raised to life for our justification. (Rom 4:25)**
>
> **Who is he that condemns? Christ Jesus, who died—more than that, who was raised to life—is at the right hand of God and is also interceding for us. (Rom 8:34)**
>
> **Therefore he is able to save completely those who come to God through him, because he always lives to intercede for them. (Heb 7:25)**

3. The third question: "Did not the prophets predict Messiah's death and resurrection?" (v.25-27). Note several facts.

a. Jesus rebuked the two disciples for being dull and slow to believe. He called them "foolish" (anoetoi), which means that they were dull and slow to believe. More was expected of them; they should have known more than they were indicating. They were without excuse, for their minds and hearts were capable of more. Therefore, Jesus rebuked them for being...
- *slow to believe*
- slow to believe *all* the prophets had spoken

b. Jesus shared that the death and resurrection of the Messiah was a necessity. The words "did not" (ouchi edei) are strong. They mean there was a constraint, an imperative, a necessity laid upon the Messiah to die and arise. He had no choice. His death and resurrection had been planned and willed by God through all eternity. Therefore, He had to fulfill the will of God, for God had ordained...
- that the Messiah suffer these things.
- that the Messiah enter into His glory. God's plan was not defeated. He conquered through the death of His Son, the Messiah.

c. Jesus explained the Scripture to the two disciples, taught them book by book, showing them the things concerning the Messiah in each book. Note the words "all the Scriptures." Prophecies of Christ are found in all the Scripture; therefore, Jesus carried the two disciples through the Scripture in a systematic way, book by book, showing them how God's purpose was fulfilled in the death of the Messiah. The two disciples could now be saved eternally, not just during an earthly reign of an earthly Messiah.

Thought 1. The two disciples were feeling hopeless and perplexed, full of sadness and despair for one very simple reason: unbelief. They had *symbolized* or *spiritualized* the Scripture and the clear predictions which Jesus had given his disciples before His death. Therefore, they could not see *beyond* Jesus' death. They were willing to accept and admire a *dead Savior*, a great prophet who had been martyred, but they had great difficulty in accepting a risen Lord. They would not believe the reports of the women, the glorious news of the living Lord.

> **But they did not believe the women, because their words seemed to them like nonsense. (Luke 24:11)**
>
> **Let us, therefore, make every effort to enter that rest, so that no one will fall by following their example of disobedience. (Heb 4:11)**
>
> **Consider him who endured such opposition from sinful men, so that you will not grow weary and lose heart. (Heb 12:3)**

3 (24:28-32) **Conviction—Conversion:** the third scene was experiencing the burning truth—Jesus is risen and alive forevermore. Note three important points.

1. The two disciples *sought* to hear more. They invited Jesus to stay with them. The words "acted as if" do not mean Jesus was play-acting. He never pretends. He would have gone on, for He never enters a life or a home without a personal invitation. The two were seeking the truth, so

they wanted Jesus to enter their home and to share more with them. (How unlike so many today!)

Jesus did enter, and He sat down to have dinner with them. He was also asked to give thanks for the meal.

2. God opened the eyes of the two disciples. They immediately knew the Lord. But note why: they had invited Jesus into their home. If they had let Him pass on, the likelihood is that they would never have known it was the Lord.

3. The two disciples had experienced a burning conviction within their hearts.

   a. The Word of God being proclaimed is what had stirred the conviction and the burning.

   > Therefore this is what the LORD God Almighty says: "Because the people have spoken these words, I will make my words in your mouth a fire and these people the wood it consumes. (Jer 5:14)
   >
   > "Is not my word like fire," declares the LORD, "and like a hammer that breaks a rock in pieces? (Jer 23:29)

   b. Their response to the conviction—inviting Christ into their home—led to their coming to know Him personally.

   > Here I am! I stand at the door and knock. If anyone hears my voice and opens the door, I will come in and eat with him, and he with me. (Rev 3:20)
   >
   > God, who has called you into fellowship with his Son Jesus Christ our Lord, is faithful. (1 Cor 1:9)

> For where two or three come together in my name, there am I with them." (Mat 18:20)

Thought 1. The two had heard the Scripture explained, and they had heard much. But they had to respond, to invite the Lord into their home before God could open their eyes and bring them to a knowledge of Christ.

4 (24:33-35) **Jesus Christ, Resurrection**: the fourth scene was proclaiming the immortal witness. The scene was dramatic. It was night, but the two rushed back to the apostles. When they arrived, they found the apostles and some other disciples already gathered together.

They were all bursting with excitement. To the shock of the two from Emmaus, the group had the same immortal witness to share: "The Lord has risen and has appeared to Simon." As they listened to Simon's experience, they were bursting at the seams, hardly able to contain themselves, waiting to share their own experience.

Finally, their time came to share their experience and the very same immortal witness: "The Lord has risen indeed."

> And you also must testify, for you have been with me from the beginning. (John 15:27)
>
> You will be his witness to all men of what you have seen and heard. (Acts 22:15)
>
> "We are witnesses of everything he did in the country of the Jews and in Jerusalem. They killed him by hanging him on a tree, but God raised him from the dead on the third day and caused him to be seen. (Acts 10:39-40)

1. The first statement: Jesus is risen	C. Jesus' Appearance to the Disciples: The Great Statements of the Christian Faith, 24:36-49 (Mk.16:14; Jn.20:19-23; 20:26-21:25)	42 They gave him a piece of broiled fish, 43 And he took it and ate it in their presence.	4) He ate
a. Jesus' first words: Peace b. Jesus' impact	36 While they were still talking about this, Jesus himself stood among them and said to them, "Peace be with you."	44 He said to them, "This is what I told you while I was still with you: Everything must be fulfilled that is written about me in the Law of Moses, the Prophets and the Psalms."	2. The second statement: All Scripture must be fulfilled a. The forewarning & utter necessity
1) The disciples were startled & frightened 2) The disciples were troubled & silently questioning what they were seeing	37 They were startled and frightened, thinking they saw a ghost. 38 He said to them, "Why are you troubled, and why do doubts rise in your minds?	45 Then he opened their minds so they could understand the Scriptures. 46 He told them, "This is what is written: The Christ will suffer and rise from the dead on the third day,	b. The spiritual insight needed to understand the Scriptures c. The particular prophecies that must be understood 1) Christ must suffer & arise
c. Jesus' proof[DS1] 1) He is flesh & bones	39 Look at my hands and my feet. It is I myself! Touch me and see; a ghost does not have flesh and bones, as you see I have."	47 And repentance and forgiveness of sins will be preached in his name to all nations, beginning at Jerusalem.	2) Repentance & forgiveness must be preached
2) He showed them his wounds	40 When he had said this, he showed them his hands and feet.	48 You are witnesses of these things.	
3) He talked	41 And while they still did not believe it because of joy and amazement, he asked them, "Do you have anything here to eat?"	49 I am going to send you what my Father has promised; but stay in the city until you have been clothed with power from on high."	3) The Holy Spirit & His power must be sent

DIVISION XII

THE SON OF MAN'S GLORY: HIS RESURRECTION AND ASCENSION, 24:1-53

C. Jesus' Appearance to the Disciples: The Great Statements of the Christian Faith, 24:36-49

(24:36-49) **Introduction**: this was the first appearance of Jesus to *all the disciples at once*. He shared the two great statements (explanations) of the Christian faith.

1. The first statement: Jesus is risen (vv.36-43).
2. The second statement: all Scripture must be fulfilled (vv.44-49).

(24:36-49) **Another Outline**: The Great Statements of the Christian Faith.
1. Statement 1: Jesus is risen (vv.36-43).
2. Statement 2: All prophetic Scripture must be fulfilled (vv.44-46).
   a. The whole Old Testament.
   b. The death and resurrection of Christ.
3. Statement 3: Repentance and forgiveness of sin are imperative (vv.47-48).
   a. The place: Among all nations.
   b. The witnesses: You—disciples.
4. Statement 4: Power is to come upon you (v.49).
   a. The power is the Holy Spirit
   b. The power is given by tarrying (praying).

1 (24:36-43) **Jesus Christ, Resurrection; Impact of; World Response to**: statement one is that Jesus is risen. The scene took place at night—the night of the very day of the Lord's resurrection. It was a dramatic scene. The Lord had already made at least four appearances. The four appearances named were to...

- Mary Magdalene (Jn.20:14f)
- the women visiting the tomb (Mt.28:1f; Mk.16:1f)
- the two walking to Emmaus (Lk.24:1f)
- Simon Peter (Lk.24:34; 1 Cor.15:5)

The apostles (minus Thomas) and some other disciples had rushed to the known meeting place. The very air was electric. Excitement beat in the chest of every one, and minds were grasping for understanding. Wonder was beginning to overcome sadness and despair, and hope was beginning to stir great anticipation. Reports of appearances were being buzzed about and argued about. Then all of a sudden out of nowhere, into the very midst of all this, *"Christ Himself stood."* Note three things:

1. The very first words Jesus spoke to the disciples after His death: *"Peace be unto you."* This was the regular greeting of the Jews of that day, but it had a very special significance now. The disciples needed peace, the peace that only He could give. And He had now risen from the dead to give that peace to them. (See note, *Peace—* Jn.14:27.)

"But now in Christ Jesus you who once were far away have been brought near through the blood of Christ. For he himself is our peace, who has made the two one and has destroyed the barrier, the dividing wall of hostility," (Eph.2:13-14).

"Peace I leave with you; my peace I give you. I do not give to you as the world gives. Do not let your hearts be troubled and do not be afraid." (Jn.14:27).

"I have told you these things, so that in me you may have peace. In this world you will have trouble. But take heart! I have overcome the world." (John 16:33)

2. The impact of Christ's resurrection. The disciples interpreted His sudden appearance in their midst just as they had always interpreted His words—spiritually. When He suddenly appeared, the immediate thought flashing across their minds was that a spirit was appearing to them. They were...

- startled, terrified, frightened, and troubled.
- questioning.

Thought 1. Unbelievers respond to the resurrection in five ways.

1) They are startled, terrified, frightened, and troubled by the resurrection. Why? Because it means they must obey and serve Christ. If He is the *living Lord*, then man is His subject.
2) They question the resurrection, the truth of it. The idea that a man could arise from the dead is beyond their acceptance.
3) They ignore the resurrection, pay no attention to it, and count it as being meaningless.
4) They respond to the resurrection, accepting Jesus Christ as their Savior and Lord.
5) They react to the resurrection—react all the way from mild opposition and cursing to the persecution of any who bear witness to the resurrection.

3. The proof of Christ's resurrection, that He had risen bodily. The outline of the Scripture above shows the four things Christ did to prove that it really was He and not a spirit who stood before the disciples (see DEEPER STUDY # 1—Lk.24:39-43 for discussion).

DEEPER STUDY # 1

(24:39-43) **Jesus Christ, Resurrection—Resurrection, Body of**: the risen Christ was not a spirit (v.39); not a vision, a phantom, an hallucination, or any other figment of man's imagination. He was the risen Lord—bodily—not someone else nor some other spirit. His body was none other than that of Jesus, the carpenter from Nazareth. He had physically risen from the dead and His body was real. It differed, yes, but it was His body. It was perfected and no longer subject to the limitations and frailties of the physical universe and its laws; it was now glorified by the power and spoken Word of God (cp. Ro.1:3-4).

How did the Lord's resurrected body differ from His earthly body? Some idea can be gleaned by looking at His resurrected body and the glorified body promised to the believer.

1. The resurrected body of the Lord was His body, but it was radically changed. It had all the appearance of a physical body, but it was not bound by the physical world and its material substance.
   a. It was the same body, not some other body. We know this because His resurrected body bore the marks of the nails in His hands and feet (Jn.20:20, 27), and the disciples could recognize Him after close observation.
   b. It was a body that could travel and appear anyplace, at will and by thought—a body unhampered by space, time, material, or substance. When He

appeared it was suddenly, even behind locked doors (Lk.24:36; Jn.20:19).
   c. It was a body that differed enough that it was not clearly recognized at first, not until it was closely observed.
   ⇒ Mary Magdalene thought He was the gardener (Jn.20:15).
   ⇒ The two disciples walking toward Emmaus thought He was a traveler (Lk.24:31).
   ⇒ The disciples who were fishing did not recognize Him standing on the seashore (Jn. 21:4).

However, after close observation, the Lord was recognized in all these instances.

2. The resurrected, glorified body that is promised to the believer gives some additional insight into the kind of body Christ has. One of the most wonderful promises ever made to man is given in the words:

Who, by the power that enables him to bring everything under his control, will transform our lowly bodies so that they will be like his glorious body. (Phil 3:21; see Mt.13:43; Ro.8:17; Col.3:4; Rev.22:5)

For those God foreknew he also predestined to be conformed to the likeness of his Son, that he might be the firstborn among many brothers. (Rom 8:29; see 1 Cor.15:49; 2 Cor.3:18)

Dear friends, now we are children of God, and what we will be has not yet been made known. But we know that when he appears, we shall be like him, for we shall see him as he is. (1 John 3:2)

The body of the believer will undergo a radical change just as the Lord's body was radically changed. Several changes are promised the believer.
   a. The believer shall receive a spiritual body.

It is sown a natural body [soma psuchikon], it is raised a spiritual body. If there is a natural body, there is also a spiritual body. (1 Cor 15:44)

Note: the spiritual body (soma) still retains the qualities of the earthly body (soma). The same Greek word is used for both bodies. The difference lies in that it will not be a natural (soulish) body but will be a spiritual body. What does this mean? In essence, the body will be perfected; no longer subject to pain, tears, death, sorrow, or crying (Rev.14:4).
   ⇒ It is sown in corruption; it is raised in incorruption.
   ⇒ It is sown in dishonor; it is raised in glory.
   ⇒ It is sown in weakness; it is raised in power.
   ⇒ It is sown a natural body; it is raised a spiritual body.

Note that the body is the same body on earth that it will be in heaven. The body just undergoes a radical change of nature. The believer will be the same person in heaven that he is on earth, differing only in that he is perfected. Also note the strong, emphatic declaration: *There is* a "natural body", and *there is* a "spiritual body" (1 Cor. 15:42-44).

b. The believer shall receive a body that is not "flesh and blood." Flesh and blood are corruptible; they age, deteriorate, die and decay.

> **I declare to you, brothers, that flesh and blood cannot inherit the kingdom of God, nor does the perishable inherit the imperishable. (1 Cor 15:50)**

c. The believer shall receive a body that shall be radically changed.

> **In a flash, in the twinkling of an eye, at the last trumpet. For the trumpet will sound, the dead will be raised imperishable, and we will be changed. For the perishable must clothe itself with the imperishable, and the mortal with immortality. (1 Cor 15:52-53)**

d. The believer shall be given a body that will not need reproduction for continuing the (redeemed) human race.

> **At the resurrection people will neither marry nor be given in marriage; they will be like the angels in heaven. (Mat 22:30)**

2 (24:44-49) **Prophecy, Fulfilled—Jesus Christ, Death:** statement two is that all Scripture must be fulfilled. Note four points:

1. The forewarning Jesus had given in His predictions. His death and resurrection—the literal events happening just as He had said they would—should not have been a surprise. He had foretold the events and forewarned His followers. (See outline and notes—Lk.18:31-34.)

Thought 1. Scripture predicts much that is to happen in the future. However...
- some still will not accept and believe.
- some still spiritualize the predictions.

The greatest of all tragedies is that some still do not accept and believe the Lord's death and resurrection despite the irrefutable evidence.

2. The utter necessity that Christ die and arise. The word "must" (dei) means that His death was an imperative, a necessity, a constraint.

> **I tell you the truth, until heaven and earth disappear, not the smallest letter, not the least stroke of a pen, will by any means disappear from the Law until everything is accomplished. (Mat 5:18)**
> **This man was handed over to you by God's set purpose and foreknowledge; and you, with the help of wicked men, put him to death by nailing him to the cross. But God raised him from the dead, freeing him from the agony of death, because it was impossible for death to keep its hold on him. (Acts 2:23-24)**
> **As his custom was, Paul went into the synagogue, and on three Sabbath days he**

reasoned with them from the Scriptures, explaining and proving that the Christ had to suffer and rise from the dead. "This Jesus I am proclaiming to you is the Christ," he said. (Acts 17:2-3)

Note that Christ gave the three divisions of the Old Testament: the law, the prophets, and the psalms. The whole Old Testament prophesied of His coming and His salvation.

3. The spiritual insight needed to understand the Scriptures. Christ opened the disciples' eyes so they could understand.

> **The man without the Spirit does not accept the things that come from the Spirit of God, for they are foolishness to him, and he cannot understand them, because they are spiritually discerned. (1 Cor 2:14; see 1 Cor. 2:9-14)**

4. The particular prophesies were threefold.
   a. Christ must suffer and arise (see outline and note—Lk.18:31-34).
   b. Repentance and forgiveness must be preached (see notes and DEEPER STUDY # 1—Acts 17:29-30; DEEPER STUDY # 4—Mt.26:28).
   c. The Holy Spirit and power must be sent. As the disciples went forth witnessing, they were to be given the *wonderful* promise (the Holy Spirit) and power of the Father. (See outline and notes, *Holy Spirit*—Jn.14:15-26; 16:7-15 for a discussion of the prophecies concerning the Holy Spirit which Christ had given to the disciples.) Note two points.
   1) The believer was to be equipped for witnessing.
      ⇒ He was to receive the promise of the Father (the Holy Spirit).
      ⇒ He was to receive power, being clothed (endusesthe) with power.

   2) The source of the spirit and power was God.
      ⇒ Christ was to send the promise.
      ⇒ The promise was "from the Father." God gave the promise.
      ⇒ Believers had to stay, that is, wait upon the Lord and pray for the promise.
      ⇒ The promise was to come from "on high." God Himself was the Source of power for all evangelism.

> **But you will receive power when the Holy Spirit comes on you; and you will be my witnesses in Jerusalem, and in all Judea and Samaria, and to the ends of the earth." (Acts 1:8)**
> **When he comes, he will convict the world of guilt in regard to sin and righteousness and judgment: (John 16:8)**
> **Now to him who is able to do immeasurably more than all we ask or imagine, according to his power that is at work within us, (Eph 3:20)**

	D. Jesus' Last Appearance: The Ascension,[DS1] 24:50-53 (Mk.16:19-20; Acts 1:9-11)
1. **The purpose of the ascension** a. To bless His followers	50 When he had led them out to the vicinity of Bethany, he lifted up his hands and blessed them.
b. To provide a witness & give great assurance to His followers	51 While he was blessing them, he left them and was taken up into heaven.
2. **The disciples' response to the ascension** a. Worshipped Him b. Were filled with joy	52 Then they worshiped him and returned to Jerusalem with great joy. 53 And they stayed continually at the temple, praising God.

DIVISION XII

THE SON OF MAN'S GLORY: HIS RESURRECTION AND ASCENSION, 24:1-53

D. Jesus' Last Appearance: The Ascension, 24:50-53

(24:50-53) **Introduction**: Luke closes his gospel with the ascension of Christ and begins Acts with the ascension of Christ (Acts 1:9-11). The ascension closes the Lord's earthly ministry, His mission to save the world. Therefore, the ascension can be said to be the final chapter, the close, the consummation of His journey upon earth. On the other hand, the ascension opens the Lord's heavenly ministry, His mission of intercession for the world and His mission of bearing witness through the lives of believers. Therefore, the ascension can be said to be the first chapter, the opening, the beginning of His journey into heaven as the Risen Lord. In heaven, Jesus Christ is the risen Lord who is the propitiation "for the sins of the whole world" (1 Jn.2:1-2).

1. The purpose of the ascension (vv.50-51).
2. The disciples' response to the ascension (vv.52-53).

DEEPER STUDY # 1

(24:50-53) **Jesus Christ, Ascension**: the Lord ascended to the right hand of God, that is, to the position of sovereignty and power (see Mk.16:19; Lk.22:69; Acts 1:9-11; 2:36; 5:31; Eph.1:20; Ph.2:9-11; Rev.5:12). The ascension assures (proves, confirms) that seven things are absolutely certain.

1. The ascension assures that God *is*, that He is alive and does exist. The fact that Christ was raised up from the dead and "taken up into heaven" (Lk.24:51) proves that God is. Only God could do such a thing (1 Cor.6:14; 2 Cor.4:14; see Jn.3:16. See Acts 2:24, 32; 3:15, 26; 4:14; 5:30; 10:40; 13:30, 33-34; 17:31.)

2. The ascension assures that Christ is God's Son. The very fact that God raised up Christ and "was taken [Him] up into heaven" proves that Christ is God's Son (Mk.16:19; Ro.1:3-4; Ph.2:5-11).

3. The ascension assures that heaven is real (Ph.3:20-31).

4. The ascension assures that the gospel is true. When God raised up Christ and received Him into heaven, God validated the message of Christ. What Christ proclaimed and revealed was true: man faces a critical problem, the problem of sin and death and a future of condemnation and separation from God. However, man can be saved by the cross of Christ (Mk.16:16; 1 Pt.2:24).

5. The ascension assures that the Great Commission is the call and mission of believers. Two things show this. First, Christ has ascended into heaven; therefore, He is gone, no longer on earth. If the gospel is to be carried to the ends of the earth, believers have to do it. They are the ones left on earth to do it. Second, it is the risen and ascended Lord who gave the Great Commission. *As the ascended Lord*, He demands that His commission be fulfilled (Mk.16:15; see Mt.28:19-20).

6. The ascension assures that power is available to carry out the Great Commission (Mt.28:18; see Mk.16:20).

7. The ascension assures that we have a very special Helper in heaven, One who really loves and cares for us. He is One who is sympathetic with "our weaknesses...tempted in every way, just as we are—yet was without sin" (Heb.4:15). Therefore, He is ever ready to forgive and to look after us through all of life.

1 (24:50-51) **Jesus Christ, Ascension**: the purpose of the ascension. Two general purposes are given by Luke (see note, *Ascension*—Acts 1:9).

1. The first general purpose of the ascension was to bless the disciples. This was His final blessing, and note: it was the last thing He did on earth. His last gesture and act was to bless His disciples. This showed several things.

 a. It showed that He was the High Priest who had the power to make the sin-offering for them and to bless them with the gift of peace with God. (See Aaron, Lev.9:22.)

  Then Aaron lifted his hands toward the people and blessed them. And having sacrificed the sin offering, the burnt offering and the fellowship offering, he stepped down. (Lev 9:22)

 b. It showed that His blessing was the blessing coming from the ascended Lord who was *in heaven* exalted to the right hand of God.

  And his incomparably great power for us who believe. That power is like the

working of his mighty strength, which he exerted in Christ when he raised him from the dead and seated him at his right hand in the heavenly realms, far above all rule and authority, power and dominion, and every title that can be given, not only in the present age but also in the one to come. (Eph 1:19-21)
Now to him who is able to do immeasurably more than all we ask or imagine, according to his power that is at work within us, (Eph 3:20)

c. It showed that His blessing was forever, without end, even to the end of the world.

And teaching them to obey everything I have commanded you. And surely I am with you always, to the very end of the age." (Mat 28:20)

d. It showed that His blessing was unlimited, from their ascended and *eternal Lord.*

He is before all things, and in him all things hold together. (Col 1:17)
I am the Alpha and the Omega, the First and the Last, the Beginning and the End. (Rev 22:13)

e. It showed that His blessing was upon them as they went forth as His representatives, witnessing for Him.

Therefore go and make disciples of all nations, baptizing them in the name of the Father and of the Son and of the Holy Spirit, and teaching them to obey everything I have commanded you. And surely I am with you always, to the very end of the age." (Mat 28:19-20)

2. The second general purpose of the ascension was to provide a witness and give great assurance (see DEEPER STUDY # 1—Lk.24:50-53).

2 (24:52-53) **Ascension, Results**: the disciples' response to the ascension was threefold.

1. The disciples worshiped Christ. The ascension stirred worship. Why? The disciples now knew beyond question that He was the true Messiah, the Son of God Himself. He had ascended to the right hand of God; therefore, He was due all the homage, adoration, and praise due God.

Philip said, "Lord, show us the Father and that will be enough for us." Jesus answered: "Don't you know me, Philip, even after I have been among you such a long time? Anyone who has seen me has seen the Father. How can you say, 'Show us the Father'? Don't you believe that I am in the Father, and that the Father is in me? The words I say to you are not just my own. Rather, it is the Father, living in me, who is doing his work. Believe me when I say that I am in the Father and the Father is in me; or at least believe on the evidence of the miracles themselves. (John 14:8-11)
And being found in appearance as a

man, he humbled himself and became obedient to death—even death on a cross! Therefore God exalted him to the highest place and gave him the name that is above every name, that at the name of Jesus every knee should bow, in heaven and on earth and under the earth, and every tongue confess that Jesus Christ is Lord, to the glory of God the Father. (Phil 2:8-11)

2. The disciples were filled with joy.
   a. They were filled with joy because their Lord was now exalted and privileged to take His rightful place: sitting at the right hand of God and being worshiped eternally. They were filled with joy and rejoicing *for Him.*
   b. They were filled with joy because they now knew that His presence would always be with them. When on earth physically, He could only be in one place and with only a few people at a time. But now, since ascending, He could send His Spirit to dwell with believers everywhere (Omnipresent). Nothing would ever again be able to *separate* their Lord from them.

But I tell you the truth: It is for your good that I am going away. Unless I go away, the Counselor will not come to you; but if I go, I will send him to you. (John 16:7)
Who shall separate us from the love of Christ? Shall trouble or hardship or persecution or famine or nakedness or danger or sword? For I am convinced that neither death nor life, neither angels nor demons, neither the present nor the future, nor any powers, neither height nor depth, nor anything else in all creation, will be able to separate us from the love of God that is in Christ Jesus our Lord. (Rom 8:35, 38-39)

3. The disciples were in the temple continually. The temple was the focus of God's presence and worship, and it was the center of teaching, the place where the people were instructed in the Scriptures. The disciples were bound to focus their lives in the temple or church...
   • because Christ had taught that the temple was His "Father's house" and "the house of prayer."

"It is written," he said to them, "'My house will be a house of prayer'; but you have made it 'a den of robbers.'" (Luke 19:46)
To those who sold doves he said, "Get these out of here! How dare you turn my Father's house into a market!" (John 2:16)

   • because they wished to praise God for sending the Messiah and to bear public testimony of Him.
   • because the temple was the chosen place of God to manifest His presence among His people (see note—1 Cor.3:16).

"Go, stand in the temple courts," he said, "and tell the people the full message of this new life." (Acts 5:20)
Let us not give up meeting together, as some are in the habit of doing, but let us encourage one another—and all the more as you see the Day approaching. (Heb 10:25)

OUTLINE BIBLE RESOURCES

This material, like similar works, has come from imperfect man and is thus susceptible to human error. We are nevertheless grateful to God for both calling us and empowering us through His Holy Spirit to undertake this task. Because of His goodness and grace, *The Preacher's Outline & Sermon Bible*® New Testament and Old Testament volumes are now complete.

The Minister's Personal Handbook, The Believer's Personal Handbook, and other helpful **Outline Bible Resources** are available in printed form as well as releasing electronically on various software programs.

God has given the strength and stamina to bring us this far. Our confidence is that as we keep our eyes on Him and remain grounded in the undeniable truths of the Word, we will continue to produce other helpful Outline Bible Resources for God's dear servants to use in their Bible Study and discipleship.

We offer this material, first, to Him in whose Name we labor and serve and for whose glory it has been produced, and, second, to everyone everywhere who preaches and teaches the Word.

Our daily prayer is that each volume will lead thousands, millions, yes, even billions, into a better understanding of the Holy Scriptures and a fuller knowledge of Jesus Christ the Incarnate Word, of whom the Scriptures so faithfully testify.

You will be pleased to know that Leadership Ministries Worldwide partners with Christian organizations, printers, and mission groups around the world to make Outline Bible Resources available and affordable in many countries and foreign languages. It is our goal that *every* leader around the world, both clergy and lay, will be able to understand God's Holy Word and to present God's message with more clarity, authority, and understanding—all beyond his or her own power.

LEADERSHIP MINISTRIES WORLDWIDE
PO Box 21310 • Chattanooga, TN 37424-0310
(423) 855-2181 • FAX (423) 855-8616
info@lmw.org
www.lmw.org - FREE Download materials

LEADERSHIP MINISTRIES WORLDWIDE

Publishers of Outline Bible Resources

- **THE PREACHER'S OUTLINE & SERMON BIBLE® (POSB) • KJV – NIV**

NEW TESTAMENT

Matthew 1 (chapters 1–15)
Matthew 2 (chapters 16–28)
Mark
Luke
John
Acts
Romans

1 & 2 Corinthians
Galatians, Ephesians, Philippians, Colossians
1 & 2 Thessalonians, 1 & 2 Timothy, Titus, Philemon
Hebrews, James
1 & 2 Peter, 1, 2, & 3 John, Jude
Revelation
Master Outline & Subject Index

OLD TESTAMENT

Genesis 1 (chapters 1–11)
Genesis 2 (chapters 12–50)
Exodus 1 (chapters 1–18)
Exodus 2 (chapters 19–40)
Leviticus
Numbers
Deuteronomy
Joshua
Judges, Ruth
1 Samuel
2 Samuel

1 Kings
2 Kings
1 Chronicles
2 Chronicles
Ezra, Nehemiah, Esther, Job
Psalms 1 (chapters 1-41)
Psalms 2 (chapters 42-106)
Psalms 3 (chapters 107-150)
Proverbs
Ecclesiastes, Song of Solomon

Isaiah 1 (chapters 1-35)
Isaiah 2 (chapters 36-66)
Jeremiah 1 (chapters 1-29)
Jeremiah 2 (chapters 30-52),
  Lamentations
Ezekiel
Daniel, Hosea
Joel, Amos, Obadiah, Jonah,
  Micah, Nahum
Habakkuk, Zephaniah, Haggai,
  Zechariah, Malachi

Print versions of all Outline Bible Resources are available in various forms.

- ***What the Bible Says to the Believer*** — **The Believer's Personal Handbook**
  11 Chs. – Over 500 Subjects, 300 Promises, & 400 Verses Expounded - Italian Imitation Leather or Paperback

- ***What the Bible Says to the Minister*** — **The Minister's Personal Handbook**
  12 Chs. - 127 Subjects - 400 Verses Expounded - Italian Imitation Leather or Paperback

- **Practical Word Studies In the New Testament** — 2 Vol. Hardcover Set

- **The Teacher's Outline & Study Bible™ - Various New Testament Books**
  Complete 30 - 45 minute lessons – with illustrations and discussion questions

- **Practical Illustrations — Companion to the POSB**
  Arranged by topic and Scripture reference

- **What the Bible Says About Series – Various Subjects**

- **OBR on various digital platforms**
  See current digital providers on our website at www.lmw.org

- **Translations of various books**
  See our website for more information or contact our office

— Contact LMW for quantity orders and information —

LEADERSHIP MINISTRIES WORLDWIDE or Your Local Christian Bookstore
PO Box 21310 • Chattanooga, TN 37424-0310
(423) 855-2181 • FAX (423) 855-8616 (Mon. - Thurs. 9am – 5pm Eastern)
E-mail - info@lmw.org • Order online at www.lmw.org

PURPOSE STATEMENT

LEADERSHIP MINISTRIES WORLDWIDE

exists to equip ministers, teachers, and laymen in their understanding, preaching, and teaching of God's Word by publishing and distributing worldwide *The Preacher's Outline & Sermon Bible*® and related **Outline Bible** materials; to reach & disciple men, women, boys and girls for Jesus Christ.

MISSION STATEMENT

1. To make the Bible so understandable – its truth so clear and plain – that men and women everywhere, whether teacher or student, preacher or hearer, can grasp its message and receive Jesus Christ as Savior, and…

2. To place the Bible in the hands of all who will preach and teach God's Holy Word, verse by verse, precept by precept, regardless of the individual's ability to purchase it.

The **Outline Bible** materials have been given to LMW for printing and especially distribution worldwide at/below cost, by those who remain anonymous. One fact, however, is as true today as it was in the time of Christ:

THE GOSPEL IS FREE, BUT THE COST OF TAKING IT IS NOT

LMW depends on the generous gifts of believers with a heart for Him and a love for the lost. They help pay for the printing, translating, and distributing of **Outline Bible** materials into the hands of God's servants worldwide, who will present the Gospel message with clarity, authority, and understanding beyond their own.

LMW was incorporated in the state of Tennessee in July 1992 and received IRS 501 (c)(3) nonprofit status in March 1994. LMW is an international, nondenominational mission organization. All proceeds from USA sales, along with donations from donor partners, go directly to underwrite our translation and distribution projects of **Outline Bible** materials to preachers, church and lay leaders, and Bible students around the world.